Who's Going to Stop Us Now?

WHO'S GOING TO STOP US NOW?

VOLUME II
LESSONS IN LETTING GO

Meri Har-Gil

Keren Baranes Abu / Jully Black / Ruth Cohen / Marla David / Debbie Doolittle / Christie Echeverri / Angie Fix / Orit Gal / Jaime Lund Onofrey / Maria Reda Goldstein / Nell Rose Foreman

Who's Going to Stop Us Now?
Lessons in Letting Go

Copyright © 2018 by Meri Har-Gil
All rights reserved.

No part of this publication may be reproduced, stored in a retrieval system, or transmitted in any form or by any means-electronic, mechanical, photo-copy, recording, or any other-without the prior permission of the author.

ISBN: 978-0-9951591-2-9

Printed in Canada

Table of Contents

A Message from Meri 1

Introduction 3

Designing Happiness
By Keren Abu 5

The Skin I Am In
By Jully Black 15

My Life As a Dog
By Ruth Cohen 29

Heart Warrior: Time Helps But Love Heals
By Marla David 49

Choosing Happiness
By Debbie Doolittle 63

Love Is Larger Than Loss
By Christie Echeverri 75

Love Boomerang
By Angie Fix 85

Befriending Fear
By Orit Gal 95

Colouring Outside the Lines
By Jaime Lund Onofrey 109

Love is Not So Blind
By: Maria Reda Goldstein 123

Breathing Through the Changes
By Nell Rose Foreman 137

About the Authors 145

A MESSAGE FROM MERI

Ever since publishing my first co-authored book in 2015, I've dreamed of producing my own compilation. My vision was to create a series of books dedicated towards inspiring those burdened by the weight of their past, to let go and start fresh, with a new zest for life. I wanted anyone struggling with adversity to understand, they are not alone. Well, in 2016, my dream came true when, *Who's Going to Stop Us Now? Inspiring Stories Written by 15 Unstoppable Women* made its debut on the Amazon self-help Best Seller list. Through the stories depicted, we learned the only person capable of stopping us, is ourselves. In essence, we hold the power in our own hands to effect meaningful change in our lives. Two years later, I'm incredibly proud to be publishing *Who's Going to Stop Us Now? Volume II: Lessons in Letting Go.*

Bringing this book to fruition in many ways, has been my own personal lesson in letting go. Being the perfectionist that I am, it was hard for me to come to terms with the fact that Volume II wouldn't be published within the twelve-month timeframe we originally allotted. As the days and weeks turned into months, I continually came up with excuses as to why our book was only inching its way towards the finish line. I eventually realized all the justification in the world wasn't going to result in a published book. I had to learn to let go of the time that had elapsed and surrender to the process. It took a full twenty-four months from beginning to end, to complete this project. The creation of this book has given me a whole new appreciation for hard work, and the collective effort it takes to achieve a desired result. As such, there are a number of special individuals without whom, the publication of this book wouldn't have been possible.

First and foremost, I want to thank my husband Eyal. No matter the challenge, we face it together. Raising four incredible children with you has been an honour. I thank God every day I have you by my side. Thank you for your unwavering faith, love, and support.

I would also like to thank my four beautiful children. The love I feel for each of you inspires me every day to ensure I am doing my part to make this world a better place for your generation and the generations to come.

I would be remiss if I did not mention the powerful influence my mother has had on my life. Raising thirteen children in rural Israel in the 1960s was no easy feat. You are a strong source of inspiration and a true role model. I love you.

It is imperative that I acknowledge my team of editors, Ilana Coristine and Christie Echeverri, for their dedication and professionalism. The two of you have worked tirelessly putting this compilation together. Your vision, attention to detail, and innate talent is unparalleled and I am so lucky the universe brought us together. Thank you for helping bring everyone's stories to life.

I also want to thank all of my clients. My early experiences working as an esthetician for so many years allowed me the privilege of listening to your life stories and struggles. It was those pivotal moments that first made me believe I could help others on a larger scale through life coaching.

Finally, it's clear I owe a debt of gratitude to the collective effort it has taken to accomplish my goal. Thank you to all of our co-authors who were willing to share their stories with the world. I simply would not be here today without all of you.

Meri Har-Gil

INTRODUCTION

No one journeys through life unscathed. We have all experienced the pain that accompanies being human, whether it's abuse, heartbreak, death, illness, or some combination therein. Despite this, the world is not overrun with dejected souls. Why not? Aren't we at least a little entitled? How does one forgive the unforgivable, or emerge from a cocoon of grief ready to live again?

We choose. That is how. Piece by piece, and on our own timeline, we choose to harness our inner strength and play the hand we have been dealt. We choose the trajectory of our thoughts, and those thoughts become our destiny. We forgive transgressions, not necessarily for the sake of the perpetrator, but rather for our own progress.

We let go of what could have been, and we get busy living what will be.

We all possess this choice. It is an equalizer, the one thing that cannot be taken from us. People who truly find happiness know that, eventually, the cards get reshuffled and dealt anew. Life, in all its unfairness, complexity, and unpredictability, favours those who embrace its tides.

As story editors, we are extremely proud of *Who's Going to Stop Us Now? Volume II: Lessons in Letting Go*. Volume I of this series set out to inspire and empower its readers. Volume II peels back an extra layer of the proverbial onion by bringing the act of forgiveness to the fore. Freeing ourselves from the burdens that hold us back, allows us to live authentic and meaningful lives. Our eleven incredible authors embody courage and grace. They've transcribed their deepest and darkest truths in hopes of validating and helping others. At the end of this inspiring journey, you'll see that the ability to let go of pain, victimization, and shame, ultimately lies in our ability to forgive.

Ilana Coristine and Christie Echeverri

DESIGNING HAPPINESS
BY KEREN ABU

As Dad and I stood in the entranceway of the old-age home, a soft wind blew and I felt a shiver run down my spine. From the outside, the place looked nice enough. Colourful flowers and carefully manicured lawns lined the walkway leading to the front door. I knew, however, that the aesthetically pleasing façade existed only to hide the lack of warmth inside the building.

A talking parrot greeted us as we entered. Though endearing, I couldn't help but take the bird's communication as a warning to *enter at your own risk*. Then came the unmistakable stench of an old-age home wafting under our noses, foreshadowing what was to come. Dad looked at me with *I don't belong here* eyes and I glanced back in agreement. Unfortunately, there was no other option. All the other public old-age homes were fully occupied, and the private ones were far too expensive. The irony of it all was that my dad wasn't elderly. He was only sixty-one but had suffered with diabetes and poor health for the last twenty years. When my younger siblings and I made the decision to bring him here, he had just experienced organ failure and was recovering from a coma. This was the only place Dad could go to be rehabilitated and receive the medical care we couldn't provide at home.

As we gained our bearings, a friendly nurse introduced herself. "You've arrived just in time for dinner," she said, leading us to the dining room.

We took notice of the patients around us while eating. Most needed assistance with their food. By comparison, I couldn't help but think that all my father required was some minor medical rehab, certainly not the elder care that everyone else in the place needed. *Why was this the only option for him?*

Dad looked at me with tears in his eyes. "Keren, do you think this is the right place for me? It's scary here." I will never forget how innocent and helpless he seemed at that moment. Seeing my father—once so strong, protective and invincible—reduced to a dependent, frail man was more than I could bear. For the first time I saw my father broken and powerless. I was trying so hard not to let the tears escape, and to stay as strong for him as he had for me throughout the years.

"Dad, for now, this is where you need to be, just until we find a more suitable place for you." I excused myself from the dining room so he wouldn't see the storm of emotion brewing inside me.

When I left him there for his first evening alone, I ran outside as far away as I could get and screamed at the top of my lungs. *He doesn't deserve this*, I thought as I cried helplessly. I promised myself in that moment that I would never let something like this happen to me. I vowed to do everything in my power to never be in a position of having to depend on other people. Little did I know, I was already a few steps ahead of myself; I'd been laying the foundation for a successful future.

* * *

In Israel, where I grew up, every able-bodied citizen is obligated to complete two years of military service after high school. Following my time in the army, some friends and I packed our bags and went on the trip of a lifetime around the world. That year was one of the most peaceful I'd ever experienced. It was the first time I was able to leave my troubled family life behind and focus on myself. Instead of travelling with the weight of the world on my shoulders, all I had was a knapsack on my back.

When I came home, I got a job working at the airport, the closest I could get to my next trip abroad. Working there gave me a much-needed break from all the chaos I endured at home.

It was a fast-paced, young, hip environment, and I loved the distraction. From time to time after a shift, a bunch of us would go out for lunch or just sit and chat over coffee. This is how I came to meet Eitan, the love of my life. After two years of working together, we fell in love. There was no doubt in my mind that he was the one for me. He always knew how to give me the best advice at the right place, at the right time. Whenever I needed to talk he was there without question.

It wasn't love at first sight, but something in his gaze made me feel confident. He was my source of sanity when everything else was crazy. It was weird for me that Eitan had lived in the same home from the day he was born, while my family had moved more than twenty-one times in the past twenty years. Needless to say, moving an average of once per year made for a very difficult childhood. Trying to adjust over and over again to a new neighbourhood, new school and new friends was never easy. Luckily, I'm somewhat of a social butterfly.

Eitan was discerning, and very intuitive. On one of our dates he asked me, "How is it that you've been working for two years yet never have any money?" We trusted and told each other everything, but this was a topic I had tried to avoid. I didn't want him to know what my home life was like because I didn't think he'd understand, given the stable environment he'd grown up in.

With innocence, I told him, "I deposit my monthly salary into my parents' bank account. They need it more than I do. I leave myself some allowance, but I know that if I don't help, their financial situation will be much worse."

Though warm and generous, with a big heart, Eitan didn't quite understand what I was saying. He was in shock, and for a moment he thought he didn't hear me correctly.

"I understand that your parents struggle to make ends meet, but Keren, this isn't normal. How will you start your own life?" he said. "You're young, you have your whole life ahead of you, and you need to start thinking about your future. Only you can control your own destiny. Nobody else can, and it's in your power to create a better life for yourself." Talking about this with Eitan was a pivotal moment for me. I knew what he was saying was true and that I had to make a change or everything would remain the same. *But how?* I didn't exactly have the best role models when it came to managing finances.

My parents' marriage was volatile and as a result, I grew up in a very unstable home. My father loved life, lived impulsively, and didn't think about the consequences. His main goal was to have fun with his family and friends. An eternal optimist, my father took everything he did to the extreme. My father spent excessively, overate, and even loved to the depths of his soul. Although my parents didn't get along, there was never any doubt about how much my father loved my mother. Likewise, his love for his children was endless and we always knew it. My mother, on the other hand, was calculated, mindful, and more anxious in nature. She projected fear; we always knew she was worried about the family finances. If we didn't *need* it, we shouldn't have it, especially when we didn't have the money. My father, by contrast, would buy everything in excess. That's when my mother's stress would boil over and they would fight. She always took care of our basic needs, making sure we were fed, that we studied, were taught good values, and had a moral compass to follow. Dad's priority was loving us.

Our parents' relationship unstable, but our financial situation was even worse. The more they disagreed, the more debt we incurred. With every passionate fight they'd have, my father would storm out of the house. This made my mother extremely upset, and at a very young age I became her shoulder to cry on. As the oldest child, I was the one my mother leaned on most. She'd walk into my room and proceed to tell me how bad things were between them and how scared she was that at any moment someone could come knocking on the door asking for money owed. All I wanted to do was take away my mother's pain. But I didn't know how. Looking back, a girl of only ten, twelve, fourteen years old, shouldn't have to deal with the fear of her parents' decisions.

My father spent more money than he made, and as such could never pay his bills or even afford our basic necessities. This reckless behaviour resulted in us having to run away from his creditors. Eventually they found us. In Israel, as in many countries, if you couldn't afford to pay your debts, the government would seize your assets, including the contents of your home. One beautiful sunny day, just prior to summer vacation from school, I came home to a scene I will never forget. I was in grade seven and my family had been living in the same apartment building for almost two years, the longest we'd ever stayed in one place. I had developed a routine of playing with friends who lived in our building after school. We'd all drop our bags off inside and run back downstairs to play. Those were the days with no Internet, and no cell phones—just pure, innocent play.

As I arrived home from school that day with a good friend, I was shocked to find the contents of my house gone! I had walked inside just as the last remaining item was making its way out the door. That item was a bookshelf which had been safely grounded in my bedroom. Somehow it had represented stability in my life for the mere fact that it hadn't been moved in two years. Now it was gone. I froze once I saw that everything in the house had been confiscated. I knew what it all meant and I thought to myself, *No, please, not again.* I didn't want to start my life over in a new house, with new neighbours and a new school. I didn't want to apologize to my friends for leaving without warning. The hardest part that day was seeing them outside our building, waiting to play with me when I came home from school. But it was over. Again.

Anger set in. I was old enough to know what uprooting my family meant. My friends didn't understand why we had to move, and my family fell victim to neighbourhood rumors. We'd hear whispers of "What is happening to this family…?" I started to feel like a victim myself. *Why was I being forced to grow up so quickly?* I was still a child; this time in my life should have been free from worry. Instead, I had to maintain a level of maturity reserved for adults. A sense of suffocation consumed me. I had no one to talk to, no one to turn to for help. I felt so embarrassed having to lie to my friends over and over again each time we moved. I couldn't tell them the truth, because how could they possibly understand my reality? As a child, my friends meant everything to me. They were my life—and to have them repeatedly taken away from me was devastatingly heartbreaking.

I can still feel the fear to this day. While I know there are others dealing with much larger issues, as a child, the hardships we experienced felt like the worst thing that could happen. The fear of living day-to-day, not knowing if we were going to have to move at any moment, was paralyzing. By constantly running from the "bad" people looking to collect money from my father, I felt exposed and vulnerable. Unbeknownst to me, the worst was yet to come.

At the age of eighteen I entered the army and was assigned to the air force. Throughout my service I continually felt torn between my family struggles and my military responsibilities. The combination of my father's inability to pay his bills and my mother's anxiety level pushed me to my limit. To supplement my family income, I took a job as a hostess in a restaurant in Tel Aviv. One day, after working long hours in the army, and a subsequent night shift at the restaurant, I came home at 1:00 AM to a feeling of distress I had never before experienced. When I opened the door my mother was crying on our couch. She had been up waiting for me to come home. Through her tears she began to explain. "Keren, I don't know how to tell you this… Dad is going to jail. He's been sentenced to a year in prison for tax evasion."

Time came to a grinding halt.

"What? Dad? But how could this be?" I didn't quite understand how he could have done something so terrible that would warrant him going to jail. Despite his shortcomings, he was my strength, the one who loved us unconditionally and would do anything for our happiness. My whole life had been filled with instability and chaos, and now they were taking my beloved dad, too.

The time my father spent in prison was the worst eight months of my life. Although he was sentenced to one year, he was released early for good behaviour. I have stored this time in my life far away in my long-lost memory bank because until now, it's been too painful to recall. Every Saturday brought heartache, as I'd pass multiple security checkpoints just to see him. This period between training in the army and helping my mother manage the household was hard, but we got through it.

When my father came home from prison he wasn't the same. His spirit had been broken and my parents' relationship turned to one of hatred. My siblings and I tried our best to keep them together, to no avail. She decided to leave him. My mother could not get over the life she never had, and my father's misguided ways. I felt powerless and unable to help them. Nonetheless, I was happy to have my dad back.

After completing my time in the army and traveling the world, I met Eitan. We envisioned a better life, but idly dreaming was never going to be enough. Together, we began attending a personal development course, focused on achieving goals and learning how to take responsibility over our lives. Almost a year later, a new way of thinking had emerged. Eitan and I wanted to do something other than go to work, go back home, sleep and repeat. We wanted to influence others and help change lives, particularly for the next generation.

No one was going to hand me anything; this I knew. So with Eitan by my side I made the very difficult decision to move to Canada. I was wrought with guilt for leaving my family, and filled with fear over the bevy of unknowns. How could I move away from my home country in favor of an unfamiliar culture, language and climate? What if karma's magic didn't work in Canada? Despite my misgivings, and with very little material means, we started over in a new land. We brought with us a notebook full of dreams, definitions and declarations of success. We were on our way.

Though the transition proved difficult, I was determined for us to succeed. By now, we had a child of our own, and I desperately did not want to end up back in Israel, living a life that mirrored my parents'. As much as I loved them, I feared becoming dependent on my children for anything. With this in mind, Eitan and I founded M.E. Contracting, a successful landscape design company. We used my marketing skills and Eitan's architectural design background to build our business from the ground up—literally! Today, M.E. Contracting has become Toronto's leading landscaping, design, and construction company. The name of our business is comprised of our daughters' first initials; M for Mika and E for Emma. Our thriving company is an achievement I couldn't be prouder of.

Every move I had made by the time I was thirty years old felt like some sort of physical and metaphorical escape. Moving to Canada, my final and most favourable move, was no exception. Admittedly, I was running away from the life I had in Israel. I've come to an understanding, however; a place of acceptance rather than victimization. My childhood adversity has given me continual strength, and the ability to adapt to new surroundings with ease. I think of the trade-off as karma. My life experiences have shaped me into the hard-working, level-headed, grounded person I am. I call these qualities my "toolbox of life," and they are attributes about myself that I do not take for granted. Without them, I may not have built the prosperous life that I enjoy today.

Successes aside, I still carry guilt over having moved so far away in my father's final years. My siblings were left to care for him as his health declined. One Friday night my sister Dana called me from Israel and said, "He's gone. It's all over." My father had suffered a heart attack, but I believe he died of a broken heart. He had never truly gotten over my mother leaving him. Even though they had been separated for a number of years, they periodically stayed in contact. The last phone call they shared was a good one. She told him that she hoped to see him recover so that he could experience life the way he wanted to live it. Five hours later, he passed away. Her kind words gave him the closure he needed.

Today, I continue to live in Canada where I strive every day to create the life of my dreams, and to do my part in making sure this world is a better place for the next generation. Although my father didn't survive to witness my success, I know he continues to protect me with pride, the way he always has.

THE SKIN I AM IN
BY JULLY BLACK

My stomach balls up in nervous anticipation as I wait to hear if my name will be called this time. It's been twenty-six years since what once lived in my imagination became my reality. I've been nominated for many awards since then. I was even handpicked to sing for the queen of England! But for some reason, awards have eluded me. Rather than let the absence of awards get me down, I decided to let go of the acceptance speech I had written when I was ten years old. I kept it alive in the back of my mind, but instead focused on my craft. I knew the only real loss was giving up on my dream, so I kept making music and getting better in the process.

But now, with the roar of cheers in the background, I hear my name called for the first time. "And the Juno Award goes to…the Unruly Jully, Miss Jully Black!" That was just the beginning. "And the Much Music Video Award goes to…Jully Black!" "And the Canadian Urban Music Award goes to…Jully Black!" "And the Notable Award goes to…Jully Black!" The streak felt surreal, and the universal love from all walks of life was even crazier.

Almost every artist says it's not about the award—doing what we love for a living is the genuine reward—but let's face it, once your name is actually called and you replay that reel in your mind of the hard work it took to get from the inner city to the podium…it does feel pretty damn good to hold that trophy up high to the sky with a big ole smile and snotty tears running down your face.

It was an honour to think that through my gift of song, I was helping rebrand the now-notorious Jane & Finch ghetto back into the beautiful, successful community we knew it to be.

Paying homage to my family's legacy was overwhelming and pretty damn cool!

All it took was my first win for me to see that I *am* more than a trophy. I recognized who loved me for what I did versus who loves me for who I *am*. You see, we artists, celebrities, musicians, and creatives are people, too. We cry and we hurt, too. We're lost and we need help, too. Despite all the success of touring and TV, selling hundreds of thousands of records, being handpicked to sing for the queen of England, and even honoured by CBC Music as one of the 25 Greatest Canadian Singers Ever, I still didn't feel comfortable in my skin. I loved my body, but hated my skin. You probably think I'm referring to my race, but I'm not. The skin I am referring to was comprised of my past. It was the secret I was carrying as I became more and more famous. I was one of "them," and I didn't know how to let it go.

Today, I love the skin I'm in. Making this bold statement at age thirty-nine is my personal confirmation that there truly is a God. But as strong, powerful, courageous, beautiful and confident as I stand now, this was not always the case.

As a little girl I used to constantly ask, "God, why did you make me so tall?" I hated my height. HATED it! You could always find me in the back row in school pictures, from junior kindergarten, right until grade six. Being five foot ten inches tall at the tender age of ten wasn't the easiest body to carry around, especially when *all* your friends were average ten-year-olds, not only in height, but also in their level of maturity. I was born the youngest of nine children with twenty years between the eldest and me, so you can imagine the conversations I overheard when my brothers and sisters thought I was sleeping. I didn't show what I heard but I surely repeated it!

My low self-esteem continued for years and only worsened by the time middle school came around. By this point, I had realized that I was practically invisible to all the cute boys. In grade five I had a huge crush on Sheldon Fletcher. He was biracial and had beautiful curly hair, green eyes and cocoa skin. The day he asked me to be his girlfriend was the first time I felt likeable or even lovable. We shared lunches, sat beside each other in class, and on the bus when we went on school trips. I even sent him the old-school classic *Do You Love Me?* letters with *Yes*, *No* or *Maybe* boxes to check off his choice. I got a *Maybe*, but he did end up being my boyfriend for one whole week! In my mind, I was Mrs. Jullyann Inderia Fletcher.

It's crazy to think about the little girl I was. It blows my mind even today because it's now so clear that many of the personal decisions I made as an adult were direct reflections of the lonely little girl I was.

How I wish I could go back in time and tell my ten-year-old self how important I was and how much more graceful my little spirit would become. It would go something like this:

Dear ten-year-old self,

You are beautiful. Yes, all five foot ten of you. Top to bottom, left to right, ALL of you. I know you don't look like your average ten-year-old, but God made you extraordinary for reasons you will come to know when you're older. You don't have to measure your beauty against anyone else.

Oh, one last thing: Always remember that the opinions of others should never determine your self-worth.

Love,
39-year-old Jully

I think it's only fair that I help you understand what I looked like back then. At age ten, I wore a size ten women's shoe and I also wore a size ten in pants and dresses. The shoes my mom bought for me were so ugly that I dreamed of being born into the Asian culture, where my feet could be bound and trained to be a nice size six-to- eight.

I was like, "God, what's with these hooves? What's with the size and shape of these nostrils you gave me? Why is my hair so coarse? What's with this overbite?" Need I go on?

What's amazing is that *nobody* knew that I felt this way. I kept it between God and myself. From the size of my butt (which people now pay upwards of $20,000 to replicate), to the prominent space in my front teeth, to the surgery scars on the inside of each of my knees, I felt like a hot mess! Because I was raised in a strict Pentecostal church, I was 100% convinced that my knee surgeon was given clear instructions to botch my knees, thus ensuring that I would never get any attention from teenage boys or even have a non-church love life when I grew up! I'm telling you, that surgeon must have worked for the church that I attended to as a child. Overly dramatic, right?! That was me—dramatic Jully. The sky is falling; the sky is falling just like Chicken Little thought.

Singing became my virtual tree house, my escape. Whenever I felt happy or sad I would sing. At first my sisters would constantly yell, "SHUT UP, JULLY! STOP MAKING ALL THAT NOISE!" Little did they know that in time all that noise would become beautiful music, helping to soothe many people's souls. At six years old, my sisters enrolled me into the children's ministry as a means to channel the vocal noise I made at home. Soon enough, I stepped up and sang the lead in a complicated and soulful song. When I look back, I see that experience as the launching pad for me to become the powerful singer I am today. It enabled me to help many children avoid discouragement when they feel misunderstood, especially in the arts.

I eventually became a good athlete, which helped me lose some of the baby fat that gave me a certain level of popularity in elementary, middle and high school. As a result, I was able to leverage enough self-esteem in my adult life to sing outside of church.

Alongside love, music is the second universal language. I can certainly attest to that because music is what helped me gain (what I thought) was acceptance from my peers. The irony is that they were equally as excited for me to accept them, and I just didn't know it. By now I was in ninth grade, a star athlete thanks to my size (the same size I hated). I was seen as an asset to the basketball, volleyball and track and field teams. My athletic ability, coupled with having hands down *the* best singing voice in school, catapulted my popularity to new heights. I had an uncanny knack for mimicking A-list pop superstars of the 1980s and '90s, such as Whitney Houston and Mariah Carey. Yes, that's right honey, Jullyann Gordon was now Miss Popularity!

I was getting curvier and curvier, which led to both wanted and unwanted attention. The undesirable attention came from the mean girls in school, the "fast" boys in church, the older guys in my school, and some men in my neighbourhood. All of that made me very uncomfortable and unfortunately, my newfound status wasn't enough to shake my insecurities. That little voice of self-doubt kept rearing its ugly head.

Since I could now fit into my sister's clothes, I did the classic outfit change in the washroom when I arrived at school. I wanted to fit in with the cool girls. These girls all had older boyfriends who picked them up after school and drove us all to the mall. They bought us whole Pizza Pizza pies or McDonald's and then we'd race home before our mothers returned from work.

I remember walking home after school with my girls one hot summer day and someone asking if I had had sex yet. I was shocked into a dry mouth and I replied, "Not yet, have you?" She proudly replied, "Um yeah, most grade niners have and it feels so good. It's almost like an extreme having to pee sensation but in a good way." That didn't sound good to me, but since I was numb, confused and embarrassed at the same time, I let it be. I hadn't even thought about sex. I was a Christian girl; I'd burn in Hell if I had sex before marriage. That's fornication according to the Bible. But I couldn't lie either, because that was also a sin. Lord help me. I figured I might have to do it and ask for forgiveness after.

Now that I had a boyfriend who *all* the girls thought was the cutest guy in the neighbourhood, I was giving some thought to joining the "I ain't a virgin no more" club. I was the youngest in our fourteen-year-old clique and maintained my virgin status without feeling any pressure, because everyone was well aware of my limitations. I firmly believed that if I cursed, stole or even drank a drop of liquor I would be on a first class flight to Hell! Yes, Hell. The Devil's Mansion. To this day, I'm still a devoted Christian, but I have a clear understanding of what religion is versus what having an amazing relationship with God should be. I'm happy to declare that God is still my everything and He loves me in spite of all of my wrongdoing. After all, things don't always work out the way you intend, even when making promises to God.

Predictably, I gave into the self-imposed pressure, and at fourteen, I lost my virginity with my boyfriend. I hated it. I could barely walk. I couldn't sit evenly, and what's worse, I lied to my girlfriends about it being the best thing since sliced bread.

We skipped school and went to his house since no one was home during the day. We kissed. That was cool. He fingered me for a bit. That felt good. Then he basically rammed his penis into my vagina without stopping as I screamed at the top of my lungs. And just like that, I gave my innocence away to an unworthy young man who was seven years older than me. I went through all of that just to be a member of the "cool" club. I had to use some ice cubes to cool my swollen vagina off during the week it took for me to heal and not cry when I urinated.

Now that I was no longer a virgin, it was like the smoke signals went out to predatory men. Well, one in particular—my neighbour. The very first time he chased me and pulled on my pants I actually thought he was playing a game. It wasn't like he tore off my clothes and I "got away," so it didn't seem sexual at all. But the next time he saw me in the hallway as I passed his door he chased me again and this time he pulled me down the stairs yanked my pants and panties down, bent me over, and literally forced his penis into my vagina. Now that I wasn't a virgin, I wasn't sure if this was just sex, rape, or child sexual abuse… Like my now-former boyfriend, my neighbour was six years older than me, so was this even wrong, I wondered?

I still asked God why this had to happen to me. I know everyone says I was "big for my age," but I was still only fourteen years old. The feelings I was having were confusing because even though I stepped outside my faith and had sex, deep down in my heart of hearts I felt that what he did to me—what he continued to do—was dead wrong. As kids, our parents told us to say we were cousins, so if we were supposed to be related why would he even want to do that to me? Plus, he was so many years older than me. I felt dirty. He kept grabbing me again and again, and even took me downstairs to the supply storage area of our apartment complex.

This abuse unfortunately continued for almost two years, but it stopped immediately when I made up my mind that it was time to fight. Yes, FIGHT. I knew his pattern but he wasn't prepared for my power! On this day I declared I would no longer be his sex toy, and that this was my day to become free, at least physically. When he tried to grab me, I pushed him and then kicked him with all my might, right in between his legs. I crushed his testicles and he hit the ground so hard I thought I had killed him. I left and I never saw that door fly open as I walked past his house again! We did see each other for five years following the abuse but by now he knew, and I knew *"I can do all things through Christ who gives me strength." Philippians 4:13 NKJV*

For twenty-two long years I carried the shame of that era on my back and in my heart. It unknowingly impacted some of my most precious intimate relationships. One Sunday, I awoke with the burning desire to be free. I was an award-winning singer/songwriter, a musical pioneer in the Canadian music industry, dubbed Canada's Queen of RnB/Soul, a motivational speaker, a healer and a life coach, a victor and survivor, plus so much more. I had come so far. It was time to let go and forgive the man who had victimized me as a child. I had been on a public journey of self-discovery, and I was being called upon by various organizations to motivate women and girls to love the skin they were in. My message was one of multi-faceted acceptance—loving their family skin, their cultural skin, their actual skin, their educational skin, their spiritual skin, their health skin, their personality skin, their experience skin, their career skin—*all* of their life skin.

I was smokin' these keynotes with love, power, humility and grace even though I carried such deep pain about being abused. It's as though God gave me just enough "reserve to serve." One thing I know for sure is, when you are committed and dedicated to living a life serving others and helping them heal, you also reap the benefits, thus going from teacher to student. But when times get hard, who are the counsellors, counsellor? Who are the pastors, pastor? Who are the rabbis, rabbi? Who are the motivators, motivator? Who are the coaches, coach? Even doctors need doctors! I needed someone, too.

The day I was set free seemed like a typical Sunday afternoon. I did some grocery shopping and laundry before packing my empty Tupperware dishes and heading to Mom's for a traditional Jamaican Sunday dinner. Mom cooks like it's Christmas every week! My favourite meal is curry goat, rice and peas, callaloo, Mom's homemade potato salad and rum cake. Every week we celebrate the gift of life, love and family!

It wasn't always this way. Our tradition was made permanent when my older sister Sharon passed away unexpectedly. She was only twenty-four years old, and I was twelve. At the time of her death, she left behind a two-year-old little boy and had just given birth to a beautiful baby girl. I know Sharon is our family's guardian angel, and so rather than mourn our loss, we have chosen to celebrate her abundantly beautiful life. We all believe that her passing was a true wake-up call for our family to love harder, hug tighter, laugh louder and dream bigger, because all we have is now.

With the burning desire to share my truth, I'm almost ready to head to Mom's. My belly starts to hurt and I start having faded flashbacks to the many times my neighbour raped me. I had recently heard through the grapevine that his niece was brutally raped by a neighbour in the same complex we had lived in. This news prompted me to call my abuser's sister, with whom I was close, and confess the secret I had been carrying all these years. My hope was that I could bring her some comfort in how to deal with her own child's horrendous experience. I picked up the phone, dialled her number, and then hung up. Then I took a deep breath, said a little prayer for the right words, and dialled her number again.

The phone rang a few times when finally I heard her voice say, "Hello?" I immediately began by offering my support to her and her daughter. I knew that as when these things happen, it impacts the entire family in ways most people don't really understand. She was calm and thankful. I then proceeded to ask if I could share something very personal and painful with her that I felt only she would understand. She lovingly said, "Of course you can."

I was aware that she had been estranged from her brother (my former abuser) for many years, so I felt safe revealing this truth as a step towards forgiving him and releasing myself of the burden I had been carrying. I had also prepared a letter for her brother and saved it as a draft. I let him know that "I forgive you and release you with love." You see, forgiveness isn't for the other person; true forgiveness sets free the person who is holding the pain, shame, guilt, fear, and resentment. And boy, was I ever ready to be free!

With a huge frog in my throat and a knot in my belly, I told her how her brother had molested me for almost two years and that it had begun when I was fourteen. Instead of the sympathetic answer I expected, she instantly said, "What are you doing? Trying to gain new fans?" Then she proceeded to speak at the top of her lungs, alerting their mother, "Jully is saying my brother molested her!"

Heavy tears rolled down my face. She called her sister on a three-way call and said, "Guess what? Jully is saying our brother molested her." Then she laughed and laughed. Can you believe she laughed at me? Her final reaction was, "I heard you're writing a book. Keep on lying to gain sales." I told her I was sorry to have disrupted their family bond and let her know that a book wasn't in place—that I truly just wanted to be free. Adding insult to injury, she called her brother before I could send my letter, so he was ready and waiting with a reply. He threatened to sue me for defamation of character if I went public with my story. Twenty-two years later, this is how it went down.

Even though that conversation didn't go the way I'd hoped, I was still one step closer to being set free.

"So if the son sets you free, you will be free indeed." John 8:36

I grew up hearing our pastor quote that Bible verse as a child, but didn't understand or even know how to apply it until now. I was prompted to pray after that humiliating ordeal and upon completion, I heard a little voice say, "Tell Chantelle what happened to you and ask her if she was molested as well." Chantelle is my closest niece and the daughter of my deceased sister, Sharon. She was raised by my mom and has an old soul.

At this point, my thirty-four-year-old self was feeling afraid again; worried that I would be labeled as a teenage whore. What if my family responded in the same manner that my neighbour did? Chantelle looked up to me, and I knew I had to confide in her in case she was too afraid to share similar abuse herself. My strategy was to bare my wounds as an act of strength, and a means to give her a safe space. Although the other phone call went badly, my heart knew that at twenty-four, Chantelle was both old enough and mature enough to show me the kind of love and compassion I desperately needed. Plus, this was also my stepping-stone towards telling my mother.

As I wavered on telling her the truth, that little voice of shame kept fading in and out of the background, like the beginning of a song on the radio. "Get out of my head, devil! I will not give you permission to invade my thoughts!" I continued, "God, as I journey back to wholeness, I vow to use this experience to help as many people—women, girls, men and boys alike—to also be set free! In Jesus' name, Amen!" I often invoke the power of prayer to replace my negative thoughts, so those emotional weeds won't take root.

It was time to tell Chantelle.

I called her and asked if she could come by for a sleepover. Even at her age, she still loved to stay over at Aunty Jully's house. When she arrived, she could tell I had been crying and asked what had happened. I told her about the traumatizing phone call. I could tell Chantelle was livid, albeit in her own calm way. In response to the bomb I'd just dropped, Chantelle's instant reply was, "Aunty Jully, you have to tell Mom and Aunty Maria."

I vehemently replied, "TELL MOM AND AUNTY MARIA?! How? When? Where?"

"At Sunday dinner when Aunty Maria comes and we're all eating, you can calmly tell them just like you told me," she said.

I asked if she had been molested by anyone and thank God, she hadn't been. With strength she said, "Aunty Jully, if that had happened to me, you're the only one I would ever tell, and I would have told you right away."

When she said that to me, I felt like I had won a lifetime achievement award for best aunty! Chantelle's faith and trust in me was by far the biggest honour I had ever experienced; she singlehandedly unlocked the personal breakthrough.

As adults, we tend to lean on what's logical to solve our problems. Through the love of my niece, what became evident to me is that if we remain open and are ready for true transformation to occur, the answers can come from any willing vessel.

I still knew it would be hard on my family because we all considered the family of the man who molested me to be a part of us. I believe that there is a clear distinction between relatives and family. Relatives are assigned to us, but we choose our family. Our families had chosen and loved each other, and remained neighbours for eighteen years in the subsidized housing complex of the Jane and Finch community in Toronto. We even attended the same church together. We laughed and cried together. This impending rift in the family was a death in its own right, but just like leaves that die off in the winter and bloom again in the spring, my faith let me see that I was on my way to becoming the beautiful flower God intended me to be.

With Chantelle holding my hand under the table, I took a deep breath and began to share with my sister and mother how I was repeatedly victimized by the nice boy who lived next door. What happened once turned into multiple days, which turned into weeks, which turned into months, which turned into almost two whole years of unprotected sex anywhere he could drag me. Every time he penetrated me I saw my self-worth, self-esteem, dignity, self-love and even my place in Heaven dissipate. As I continued to share what had happened to me, I could see the tears begin to stream down all of our faces in unison. Our Sunday dinner was quickly getting cold as my courage increased and freedom started to rise.

My mother asked me why I took so long to share this with the family. I had to tell her for the first time that because I had lost my virginity the same year, I felt I was to blame for allowing him to do this to me. I also let her know that because we had just lost Sharon and now had the babies to take care of, I felt like this would have been just another burden on the family. I sensed that Mom now wanted to know what happened to take the pain away from me. I told her the modified version because I could tell she was in immense pain herself; that wasn't the intention of the conversation.

With tears running down her face and a shaky voice, Mom cried out, "Lord have mercy, he's lucky you didn't tell me when you were young, because your mother would have been serving a life sentence for murder. And if your father was here, he would have chopped him up, too!" I started to laugh because Mom is always so dramatic. It's as if God had sent some comic relief for us all. She was also livid at the length of time he abused me. I let her know that it was because I trusted him as a "cousin," and that at one point I thought the abuse was never going to end, but as I grew older and got more mature and confident, I realized that I had the power to end this abuse, and it had to start now! I first declared, "I am NOT what is happening to me," and from that declaration I birthed the strength I needed to muster up the courage and FIGHT, just like my Mama taught me. Only this time, it wasn't in the schoolyard, it was in the neighbours' basement.

My family took this revelation extremely hard, and it was even harder on my mother because she felt like she should have protected me more. I affirmed to her that she was the best mother ever, because she allowed me to come to her even now, and she was helping me find peace by excavating my broken pieces. I can now confidently say that *in the past* I was sexually abused by my neighbour, and that it is no longer about what happened to me, but rather the forgiveness and love that is happening through me for myself, my family, my friends, my fans, and now *you*!

> *"It takes courage to let things go, things that hurt you, things that wounded you, things that made you bleed and where you suffered loss. Promotions you didn't get, houses you lost, men who left you and women who betrayed you. It*

takes courage to let it go. You have to have enough faith to believe that what is in front of you is greater than what was behind you. If you don't learn how to forgive, you can never live. You cannot thrive, you cannot move forward and you will always suffer. But if that thing is still living in your head, it will still be living in your life. If you are bitter in your head, you're going to be bitter in your life. You have to make a decision that if you want more in your second half of your life than what you had in your first half of your life then you are going to have to let the first half go."

– TD Jakes

MY LIFE AS A DOG
BY RUTH COHEN

Have you ever observed the behaviour of a stray dog? The way it cowers in concealed corners and avoids human contact? The way it searches for food, rummaging through garbage cans, devouring half-eaten sandwiches or morsels of bacteria-infested meat strewn along the sidewalk? The way it guzzles water after a rainfall that's collected near a gutter? Strays tend to live on the fringes of society and are distrustful of people. Self-preservation is their first and foremost priority. That is the story of my life; yet my story is not one of defeat, despair or victimization. My story is one of triumphant strength, courage, and survival. It is the story of someone who has been thrown insurmountable roadblocks yet has had the courage to overcome them with grace and dignity.

My fate was sealed before I was born. Coming from a mixed background, I grew up with this sense that I didn't quite belong anywhere. My mother was born in Montreal post WWII, to ultra-orthodox Jewish parents - my beloved Bubby and Papa. My sperm donor, as I usually refer to him, was a Roman Catholic French Canadian with only a grade eight education. For the sake of this story we'll call him William. William was a cop who had picked up my mother while *working the beat*. To my maternal grandparents, he was the lowest of the low - a real uneducated "goy". Likewise, in his circles, William was criticized for marrying, "a dirty Jew." My mother, a Polio survivor who blamed her own mother for getting sick and losing partial use of her legs, would have done anything to escape her family of origin and distorted perception of the Jewish religion. Subsequently, I grew up as a social outcast with few to no friends and was made to feel like a complete freak. People in my Jewish community looked at me as a "shiksa", a derogatory term used to describe a non-Jewish female. However, in my mind, I was even less than that. There was no doubt I was nothing more than an unwanted mutt. Not only did I feel like an outcast in my community, but I also felt unloved by the very people who brought me into this world.

William was a man who preyed on the weak and vulnerable. He knew from the moment he met my mother that she would make an easy target given her physical disability. Her severe lack of self-esteem gave way to his abusive nature, and although she was a victim of domestic violence, she was anything but innocent when it came to raising her children. My mother had lost her first born child who didn't make it to see his first birthday. Permanent postpartum depression set in shortly thereafter. I was born next and somehow she blamed me for her first son's death. From day one, my mother rejected me, and in turn, so did William.

Beatings and Buffers:

The only time William acknowledged my existence and seemed genuinely happy was when he saw open lacerations. I spent seven years of my early childhood on the receiving end of his "red leather belt" symbolizing the exsanguination of blood – hoping that it would result in, "death like the first one." My earliest memory is from when I was two years old, standing up in my crib with an outstretched arm, reaching for my bifocals. Shortly thereafter, the thrashings began. There was no way of predicting what would set him off. He beat me as often as he felt the need. Over the years, I was whipped with various implements, sustained multiple concussions and broken bones, and spent as many hours in the emergency department of the Jewish General Hospital in Montreal as my peers spent in the dance studio or on the ice rink.

My mother had rough pregnancies and even more challenging deliveries. So when my youngest sibling David was born, my parents hired an English au pair, Melanie, to look after all three of us. In the weeks following David's birth, Melanie watched over my younger sister, Joy and I, and quickly became like an older sibling to us. She was kind, gentle and didn't make me feel invisible. One night after visiting hours at the hospital had ended, William called home. Unfortunately, I was the one who answered the phone. I could usually tell from his tone when he was out for blood. Knowing he was on his way home, I had time to prepare. My first thought was to protect Joy so I made sure that Melanie played with her, while I hid in my bedroom. Upon his arrival he barged into my room like a raging bull. He didn't even bother to take off his shoes or jacket. Being out of sight only heighten his anger. He turned everything upside down looking for me, completely destroying my perfectly made bed and throwing all my toys off the shelves and onto the floor. He eventually found me curled up like a fetus in the corner, inside my closet, hidden behind the lowest rack of clothes. He grabbed me by my long blonde hair and back-fisted me, which sent me hurling into my chest of drawers. I stood up, my head slumped over as he said, "I hate you! You should've died like the first one!" With those words he whipped his belt in the air as if it was a lasso and struck me across the head with the buckle. I fell to the ground where I remained unconscious for what I was told to be several minutes, until Melanie found me.

There's no shortage of horrific childhood memories. One in particular occurred December 1976, on our second and final road trip from Montreal to Florida. We hauled a Prowler trailer, attached to our burgundy Chevrolet Caprice Classic station wagon, complete with faux-wood paneling and a rooftop luggage rack. Both my parents were chain-smokers. En route down south, Joy, four years my junior, had an accident. We pulled off to a Welcome Centre so that she could be changed and cleaned up. My mother left me alone in the car with David and William, who was annoyed that the car reeked from her accident. David slept soundly in his car bed, untethered in the middle row. I jumped up front; a novelty for a young child to sit in the front seat. William mumbled something under his breath and then, with fire in his eyes, extinguished his lite cigarette on my exposed knee, singeing my skin, causing it to bleed and blister. I was in so much pain I could barely breathe. By the time my mother returned to the car with Joy, I had retreated to the back seat. The focus became "making up lost time" they had spent cleaning up Joy at the Welcome Centre. I was in acute agony; my charred skin hanging from my knee like a lizard shedding its scales, yet I couldn't speak. I had been muzzled by fear. All I could do to numb the pain was transport myself into the loving arms of my Bubby; my only childhood saviour.

I was fortunate enough to have a very nurturing grandmother, my Bubby, as a buffer in childhood. She taught me about resiliency before I could label it as such. After Papa died of lung cancer in March 1974, she needed comforting as much as I needed protection. We needed each other. I was only five years old when he died, but I remember my Papa as the kindest, most generous person, and his death left an enormous void in our family. Bubby and Papa were the best of friends. Every aspect of their being was intertwined. After Papa died, Bubby became my unofficial guardian every weekend, from Friday at sundown until Sunday morning when I was picked up and taken to dance. Ballet too was an escape. Apparently, I had an innate talent, but talent or not, I immersed myself so intently in ballet that it, together with Bubby's support, gave me the strength to survive my father's violent beatings.

Animal Cruelty:

In the summer of 1978, my parent's conflict at home escalated. William's rage became uncontrollable and explosive. One night, long after Joy and I had gone to bed, we woke up to the violent sounds of ceramic smashing on the floor. He was screaming at my mother about her inadequacies as a wife and mother. He was belittling her physical appearance associated with being a Polio survivor and beating her up as if she was nothing more than a punching bag. Joy pretended to be asleep, however, I could hear her whimpering beneath her covers. I desperately wanted to be at my Bubby's house or rendered invisible. I was thankful that I was not the victim of his fury that night, which destroyed the contents of our apartment like a disastrous hurricane. Then, without warning or provocation, he barged into our bedroom and ordered Joy and I to, "Wake up! Your mother wanted to kill David." Paralyzed with fear I could not move. *Please God let me wake up from this nightmare. What did he mean? Was my baby brother dead? Am I next?* I slowly crept into my parent's bedroom. Shards of glass were strewn all over the floor. My mother's 16th birthday gift from my Papa, a beautiful black-lacquered armoire accented with mother-of-pearl, was smashed into a million pieces. The mirror over her dressing table, broken. Picture frames knocked over and the family photos shredded beyond recognition.

As I tried to tiptoe out of sight, he reached up into their walk-in closet and pulled down a dusty shoebox. In it contained a handgun from when he worked as a cop. He pretended to insert bullets and then laughed as he pointed it at my mother, playing Russian roulette. I thought, *This is it. Tonight, I am going to die.* Strangely though, I did not fear death. I feared not being able to protect Joy. *And what about David? Was he already dead?* In the aftermath, I found out that what William really meant was that my mother had contemplated aborting her pregnancy when she found out she was in her first trimester with David. My mother had a string of failed pregnancies – which resulted in multiple miscarriages. I suppose she was worried about not being able to carry to term. After that, my mother courageously filed for divorce in September 1978. She told me on the way to ballet on a Thursday night. I remember feeling a sense of relief and hopefulness that my pain could finally heal with William out of my life. I would be afforded a new beginning. A chance to make friends at a new school. To be seen as something more than a human punching bag. Sadly, I never got the opportunity.

In elementary school, I was a social outcast. Up until the end of grade four, I don't remember having anyone to talk to or play with. I remember feeling very alone. In my formative years, the other kids wanted nothing to do with me. I was often absent from school for "medical reasons" only to return with visible signs of bruising or lacerations. My injuries consistently went unnoticed.

My parents' divorce was the catalyst for me switching from a French immersion school to a parochial school. I entered Talmud Torah in September 1979 when I was in grade five, where I remained until grade seven when we moved to Toronto. Up until grade five, I had been in French immersion which meant my French was at a level far beyond those of my peers and my English was well below grade level expectations. To make matters worse, I didn't speak a word of Hebrew. They put me in a grade one classroom for Hebrew, while I tried to play catch-up with English. When I entered grade six I was taking grade two Hebrew. Even though there was a clear explanation as to why I was behind in English and Hebrew, the teachers nonetheless still questioned my intellectual capabilities and used terms like, "mentally retarded" to describe me. Yet, all their bullying and insults didn't compare to the abuse I sustained at home. All I could do was pray for someone to save me; for someone to recognize that I was being beaten, since I was too afraid to tell anyone myself.

After my parents finally divorced, my mother's manic-depressive condition worsened. She became emotionally overwhelmed being saddled with the onerous responsibility of raising three children ages two, five and nine without any child support. Her hostility manifested in extreme psychological and physical torture of me. My relationship with my mother drastically changed from that of discipline, into a lifestyle of torture and torment that escalated out of control. It became so bad at times, I had no strength to crawl away, even if it meant saving my life. As a young child, William was responsible for disciplining me. After the divorce, my mother decompensated. Her maltreatment of me intensified, but I could never anticipate what would set her off. I walked on eggshells, scared to breathe too loudly or even eat too much. As abusive as the beatings were, it was her unpredictability that I feared most. Yet, for some reason, I held on to the fantasy that one day, my mother would become a "real mom" - one who nurtures and takes care, who loves unconditionally and provides the necessities of life.

As my mother's manic tendencies worsened, she started using food as a weapon of torture. She would often "forget" to feed me breakfast and send me to school without lunch. My only hope for a decent meal was at dinner, likely because she would have had to explain herself to my brother and sister as to why I wasn't eating. After returning home from school, I had a list of chores, two hours every day Monday to Friday. I was not allowed to do homework, watch TV, or go outside to play with friends until all of my chores were completed, and to her satisfaction. By the time dinner was served I was so hungry my stomach growled as if I were an angry wolf. I often stayed awake at night thinking *maybe tomorrow I'll get breakfast*. Hours later, I would drift off to sleep, dreaming about food.

In Talmud Torah, I learned how to satisfy my hunger at school. I started rummaging through the garbage cans once my classmates were outside. When I first entertained the thought of scavenging through the garbage can for scraps I felt nauseous. However, the more I thought about it, the better it seemed. I knew it was my only hope for food before dinner.

Each lunch hour at school, my stomach coiled with a combination of fear and anticipation. Anticipation because I knew that within seconds, I would have something to put in my stomach, even if it was someone else's half-eaten sandwich, cookie, or over-ripened banana. Fear because I also knew that I could get caught. In the beginning, I felt ashamed and embarrassed. Over time, it became a survival strategy. While my classmates were playing outside, I would ask to go to the washroom, and deviate inside to my homeroom, heading directly for the garbage can. I gobbled the food as fast as I could. Often swallowing pieces whole without chewing. As the weeks rolled into months, and as the pickings became slim I worked up the courage to start stealing food from my peers. While everyone was outside playing, I helped myself to whatever was left over in their lunchboxes. I got away with it for two years, until my principal caught me red-handed and asked me why I didn't have anything of my own for lunch. I don't recall exactly what I said, but I remember feeling petrified that he would call home and speak with my mother. That principal, like others who came before him, from teachers to ER doctors, never probed. They never stood back to look at the big picture or see what was right in front of them. It amazed me how nobody ever noticed that I was routinely coming to school unfed, with no lunch, exhausted, and suffering from severe sleep deprivation. *How did I continuously slip through the cracks of society?*

By the time we moved from Montreal to Toronto in December 1981, for all practical purposes, I was no longer a member of the family. I existed, but I was the cancer who needed to be extracted. I was the family scapegoat, who always got in trouble or grounded for one reason or the other. For years, I was not allowed to listen to music or talk on the phone. When I returned home from school, I was immediately presented with a list of chores my mother had assigned. When my chores were finished, I went directly to the basement, where I worked on my homework and often slept, sometimes in the unfinished furnace room, like a stray dog, because I was not well behaved and deserving of the "privilege" of sleeping in my own bed. Banned from my bedroom, my mother derived perverse pleasure knowing that I was sleeping on a concrete floor with silverfish and spiders. If I got caught sleeping anywhere else, I learned from experience there would be dire consequences.

When my mother felt my sleeping arrangements were an ineffective punishment, she changed her method of "discipline." I was not allowed to go to sleep until midnight. At age ten and eleven, I was forced to sit at our dimly lit kitchen table, shivering, praying that she would fall asleep before midnight so that I could get some rest before waking up at 6 a.m. I recall being so tired that I fell asleep sitting upright. No matter how hard I tried to stay awake, I couldn't control my head that bobbed up and down like a piece of cork in water. Once, I made the mistake of telling my mother that I was thirsty as I sat at the kitchen table. She looked at me and snickered. She pulled me up out of the chair by my ear and dragged me to the bathroom. Forcing my head into the toilet, she said, *"You're thirsty? You can drink out of the toilet like the bitch you are!"*

When I was fifteen years old, there was another horrible incident. She backed me into a corner with her arms flailing about, my head hit the wall. My mother's eyes were glazed, red with anger. I closed my eyes as the oncoming blows began to rock me from side to side. I tried to protect my face with my hands, however, my self-defense paled to her offence of attacks. Her punches seemed to last forever. Finally, I managed to snake my arm up to cover my face, to high block the oncoming jabs. My mother grabbed for my arm, but she lost her balance and staggered back. She jerked violently to regain her stability and in doing so, threw me against the railing hitting an incision site where two days earlier I had a mole removed. The outer part of my leg took the brunt of the blow. The incision opened up and I started to bleed profusely. The startled look on my mother's face told me that she had realized the severity of the situation and released her grip on my arm, and then turned and walked away as if nothing had happened. I ran to the washroom, grabbed a hand towel and applied pressure, however, I bled through the towel. That night, my mother instructed me to sleep in my bedroom, rather than in the basement. This was unusual because after a beating or a violent altercation I was always told to sleep in the basement in a sleeping bag, on the floor. The next day, she seemed deeply concerned about the condition of the incision on my leg, and drove me to the hospital. When we arrived, she told the doctor that I had tripped. The ER doctor looked at me as if to say that he knew my injury, at my age, was no accident. Once again, I was too afraid to speak up.

Embryogenesis:

"If she doesn't listen to you, I'll make her listen to you," I overheard my mother's boyfriend say one day. Well, that was all it took for me to pack my bags and leave home with whatever means possible. At the age of nineteen I left home with a suitcase in hand and nothing more than my clothes and school supplies. I rented a room with a private bath in a suburb of Toronto. I worked full-time while attending to my undergraduate courses in university. In 1994, I graduated from the University of Toronto with a Master of Social Work and began working in child protection. Although my work in this field was extremely rewarding, it wasn't until two years later, when I moved to London, England, and began working for a local authority in the Children's Social Work Department, that I was finally able to free myself from the stronghold my life in Toronto had over me. It was there that I discovered my passion for photography, gained a sense of empowerment through travel, made a friend for life and fell in love for the first time. I loved my co-workers and felt intrinsically rewarded; as though my presence made a difference – not only to the families on my caseload but to my friends, coworkers and my first love.

I left London in September 1998 because Joy was pregnant with her first child. Joy was the "joy" in our family, so it was a non-negotiable that I would leave the life I carved out for myself in the UK and come home to be by her side. Little did I know, returning home would mean stepping back into the lion's den. However, this time, I was dealing with a completely different animal.

Monsters are Real:

I married Bull in October 2000, following a two-year whirlwind courtship. The ceremony was like a fairy-tale. An intimate gathering on an exclusive sun-drenched beach in Nassau. I dove into the marriage head first fully apprised of Bull's violent temper and verbal assaults on his first wife. I thought that as a social worker if I could help my clients, I could also help him – I could "change his behaviours" and save him from hurting others. How wrong I was.

The verbal abuse and physical assaults only intensified after marriage. In May 2004, Bull head-butted me, nearly breaking my nose because of a dispute on his credit card statement. Police were called, and he was ultimately charged with assault and harassment. I was repeatedly struck with an open hand across the face. I was the receptacle for all of his verbal degradation of me as a person which completely eroded my self-worth. There's only so many times someone can be called "a bottom-feeder"; "pathetic loser"; told that I was "nothing until I met him"; "that my M.S.W. is as good as toilet paper"; ultimately culminating in Bull's determination that he will only stop trying to destroy my life when I'm "dead or end up worse off financially than before we met."

Being married to Bull was like riding a monster roller-coaster at an amusement park. For the seven years we were together, I lived the "big" life with trips down south and luxurious cruises multiple times a year. Dining out was the norm. Lavish home décor was a must. Expensive cars lined our driveway in Toronto and in our second home in Scottsdale, Arizona.

But everything has a price.

More than anything else in this world, I wanted to be a mom. That was the impetus for getting a dog in March 2001. In many respects, Dudley was my firstborn and he became my constant in life. Dudley was my keeper of secrets. He was at my side at the best of times and during my darkest of days. He saw me through a "malignant" divorce, my daughter's diagnosis with diabetes, the loss of significant friendships, entrances and exits with my mother and brother, overcoming a cancer scare, and falling on strenuous financial times – Dudley was there for all of it. He was my best friend and at times, my only friend. Dudley taught me about living each day with unbridled exuberance and delight, about seizing the moment and following your heart. He taught me to appreciate the simple things in life. When Dudley died in April 2016, I lost a piece of my lifeline. Dudley was not my whole life, however, he made my life whole.

In September 2001, I got pregnant with our daughter. My pregnancy was considered to be "high risk" given my mother's health issues, and previous miscarriages. Around 14-weeks' gestation, Bull and I had a terrible fight. I tried to remove myself from the conflict by heading into the master bedroom to fold some laundry that I had left on the bed. I made the mistake of turning my back on him which only served to inflame the situation. Like a raging bull, he raced towards me and struck the thoracic region of my back, putting stress on my lungs. I sprung forward and was doubled-over in pain. Bull picked me up and said, "Never turn your back on me bitch!" as he threw me into our bedroom wall. My shoulder ached. My legs were lifeless. I was overcome by a hot whoosh and I felt something dripping out from underneath me. The force of Bull's assault caused a tear in my placenta. I went to my OBGYN the next day and was put on bed rest for a month. Luckily the baby survived and I gave birth to my beautiful baby girl.

In May 2005, we spent a few nights in LA, en route to Hawaii from Toronto. We had just returned from a day of sightseeing. Bull always took a perverse interest in my past partners, but that night was different. There was a look in his eyes, a cunning sneer as he once again inquired about the number of men I had been with prior to him. Our daughter was nearly three years old. Bull knew that I wanted a second child.

"Why do you want more children? Do you want to make a baby tonight?" he asked.

"Not tonight. I'm not ready yet…maybe soon…I want to give our daughter someone to play with." I replied.

"Before you have more children you need to learn to be social. To be social with people and not just pets." He got up off the chair and approached the bed where I was sitting. He said, "You do something for me. I will do something for you… like normal people. Like social people. I want to give you that second child."

Bull reached down and firmly stroked the top of my head. He instructed me to unzip his pants. He looked at me and said, "…

and?" I reached inside his pants. "Now suck me with that beautiful mouth of yours," he said. I sat paralyzed with fear. I couldn't run. My daughter was sleeping in a crib nearby. The more I resisted the stronger his grip around the back of my head got. Tears began to stream down both of my cheeks. He took no notice. I tried to find the strength to fight him off, but his grip around my head was too strong. I felt like I was choking. I closed my eyes and completely detached. I pretended it wasn't happening to me.

When he got bored of that position, he threw me onto the bed, straddled my torso, and pinned my arms above my head. He then inserted his right knee into my buttocks causing my legs to fall apart, and changed his grip so that his left hand handcuffed both of my wrists. With his right hand he began to choke me; forcing his Herculean grip around my neck. He inserted himself inside of me. Pounding and thrusting harder and harder. I closed my eyes. I pretended I was anywhere but in that hotel room. Tears streamed down my cheeks. I thought of Dudley and wondered if I would ever see him again. I tried to remember the sound of Bubby's voice in the hopes it would give me the strength to fight back. I couldn't. I laid there, lifeless. He took what he wanted and then rolled over and said, "You do for me and I do for you." I ran to the bathroom, my heart pounding. I was sweating profusely and couldn't breathe. I was dizzy. I turned on the shower but I couldn't hear the water running. Everything went fuzzy. I couldn't even focus on taking the towels off the rack because I felt like my knees would buckle beneath me. I wanted to die!

The next day we went shopping on Rodeo Drive. He bought me an insanely expensive alligator handbag from Prada and then proceeded to proudly tell me that I was "amazing" the night before and although he couldn't give me another baby, he wanted to give me something as a token of his affection. That handbag never saw the light of day. Bull had previously exerted his power and dominance over me in a sexual way, but never had he dehumanized and violated me the way he did that night.

Metamorphosis:

Bull and I separated on November 7, 2005, less than a month after finding out that I was pregnant again. Bull made it abundantly clear, "I'll have nothing to do with that child. I'll pay for it as I will pay for our first child, but you'll be raising it completely on your own. Take care of the problem." Despite the immense psychological scarring associated with terminating that pregnancy which I very much wanted to keep, it was two years later, that I endured the darkest days of my life. I lost a sizable quantum of money each month in spousal support. An eight-month long parenting capacity assessment culminated in a feedback session in which the assessor said, *"I believe you were a victim of domestic violence and I believe that you are still being victimized by Bull – verbally and financially – but I am going to ignore the literature and recommend 'joint custody' with a 60/40 sharing in principal residence"*. The assessor described Bull as an *"empty vessel incapable of loving someone else"* yet in spite of Bull's noted limitations, physical custody with my daughter was reduced from 85% to 60%.

That same year, my daughter travelled with her father and stepmother to New York City over the winter break. On December 30th, my daughter called home. She was on speaker. Bull and his new wife rushed my daughter off the phone. "Why are you listening to this crap? Your mother's life is pathetic!" To protect my daughter, and minimize her exposure to the conflict, I abruptly ended the phone call. I remember lying in bed, his words resonating with my inner soul. My life was pathetic. I was a pathetic excuse for a person. A disappointment to those who knew me, but especially my daughter. I wanted to end my life. I had a plan. I would inject myself with multiple syringes of my daughter's fast-acting insulin and chase in down with a bottle of Nyquil. The next day, as everyone ushered in the New Year, I was alone at home, on the phone with the crisis distress centre. While talking to the support worker, I came to understand that no matter how many times I had been beaten, betrayed, bullied into subservience, cheated on or robbed of what was rightfully mine, I had gotten back up and fought my opponent. I had a will to survive that could not be broken.

Therapy

My life with Bull, along with my abusive childhood eventually culminated in three years of effective therapy, but it took a few failed attempts before being able to find a therapist I could be transparent with. In 2005, my therapy was court ordered after the incident with Bull which escalated to me calling the police. At that time, I didn't think I needed therapy and was offended by the therapist's suggestion that I was a victim of domestic violence. I thought, *"I was only struck a handful of times; I provoked the situation. How dare she assume to know anything about me or my husband?"* It took seven years of hearing the therapist's words in the back of my mind, *"Once should have been enough"* for me to seek help. I self-referred a social worker who specialized in treating women like me – women who were beaten by their husbands.

Social isolation with an undercurrent of depression were dominant themes in my therapy. I was resentful of my life as it was and felt invisible. *"I'm simply existing. I have no life. I am the cleaning lady, the diabetes manager, the homework tutor, nurse, life coach, social planner, and most importantly, chauffeur."* I told my therapist. Being the sole caregiver for my daughter meant I had sacrificed my freedom, friendships, having an intimate relationship with a partner or seeking treatment for my own health issues.

Therapy made me realize how difficult it is to change our behaviour. I had married my abuser because that was all I knew. Protecting myself from repeating this pattern would take significant effort to give up the familiar for the unknown. In thinking about my journey to present day, with the help of my therapist, I became willing to let go of my fake smile that hid my deepest, darkest secrets. Therapy taught me how to let go of trying to make everyone around me happy in the hopes of being included. It also allowed me to let go of the people who laughed at me when I fell down as well as those who saw me as a "victim." But by far the greatest therapeutic insight for me was learning how to let go of having expectations.

Ultimately, at the end of the three years I spent in therapy, I developed a deep appreciation for how lucky I am - to own my own home, with food in the fridge, clean clothes on my back, and most importantly, to have my daughter as my best friend.

Karate

Shortly after the dissolution of my marriage, I made the conscious and deliberate decision to register my daughter in karate. I did so for a multitude of reasons. First, to lay a foundation in self-defense so that she would never be physically assaulted or victimized. Secondly, to improve her sense of self-worth so that she would not succumb to being in an abusive, controlling relationship characterized by a marked power-differential. When my daughter entered the dojo she was an anxious three and a half year old who could not complete a class without crying. After an initial observation, the head instructor remarked that he believed my daughter lacked self-confidence and self-discipline. He said that even though she refused to actively participate in class at the outset, he felt she could greatly benefit from the program - provided we remained focused and persevered.

My daughter's tears persisted for nearly a full year. Over time, she developed strong and supportive bonds with various instructors whose nurturing dispositions enabled her to advance through the curriculum and attain black belt excellence. She overcame one obstacle after another, but she never gave up. She visualized her goal. She believed in herself despite tremendous adversity. Nothing builds self-esteem, self-confidence and the feeling of empowerment like a meaningful challenge, followed by accomplishment.

My daughter, now a second degree black belt, is a junior instructor at the dojo. She has transformed herself into a mentally and physically strong and confident individual. She is a leader amongst her peers; focused and self-disciplined. My daughter is a nurturer amongst those less able and a prime example that people who feel valued and appreciated will inevitably end up doing more than what is expected of them.

Over the years, the faces of my tormentors may have changed, as did the extent and forms of abuse that were perpetrated upon me, however, the one constant was my need to self-protect. To escape. And in doing so, I became a perfectionist. My need to be "perfect" led to obsessive-compulsive tendencies. In early childhood I lost myself in ballet. After ballet, I found acting. In adolescence, I discovered a passion in drafting original poetry. When the cathartic release from writing could no longer numb my pain, I tried to regain mastery of my environment by taking control of my weight. I hated my body. I popped appetite suppressant pills and restricted my caloric intake. In my marriage to Bull, I tried to drown out his denigrating voice and narcissistic torment by running distance. When I could no longer run, I enrolled myself in karate.

My daughter was, and continues to be a true inspiration. I had finally had enough of Bull's stronghold over me. My culture of staying silent had come to an end. I sat for over five years on the sidelines, internalizing the benefits that my daughter reaped from karate. Now it was my turn. The dojo became like my home and its instructors and fellow students like my family. Karate taught me the importance of feeling heard and being visible. It led to strong and fulfilling relationships, which allowed me to build trust. Family is usually an accident of birth, but in this case, it was a conscious decision.

Karate gave me a voice and enabled me to break my silence. It allowed me to see myself for who I am, not the victim that others made me out to be, or the victim I thought I was. The journey to black belt was one of growth and maturation. It marked the end of a chapter in my life riddled with trauma and it enabled me to become stronger in body, but more importantly, gain confidence in mind. I finally understood the difference between "victim" and "survivor". For me, it rests in "dependency". It means being able to rid myself of any sense of dependence on my abusers.

My Bubby taught me that there is no obstacle that can't be overcome. I attained black belt excellence in June 2013. I worked hard, trained with determination and persevered towards my second degree. I began a chapter in my life where I felt empowered to make changes and healthy choices and no longer felt victimized. The journey to black belt and beyond, highlighted the importance of addressing empty parts of myself associated with my traumatic childhood and further impacted by an abusive marriage. Through karate, I learnt to parent my daughter from a place of empowerment without being afraid to set boundaries. I learnt to be goal-oriented, fully present with my emotions and not stuck in a fear-based position. I owe the dojo and the people in it an everlasting debt of gratitude.

Conclusion:

I take pride in being a survivor. It's taken many years, but I have found ways to feel heard and validated. Over time, I've learned to access feelings, shed the fear, and assert myself. I've come to understand that everyone hides who they are at least some of the time. Sometimes we bury that part of ourselves so deeply we must be reminded it's even there at all. And sometimes we just want to forget who we are altogether. I suppose that's why I love Halloween. Halloween is the one time of year when everyone wears a mask - not just me. It's now time to take off the mask.

One of the most important lessons I've learned is that life is full of choices. We can choose thoughts that are inspiring and empowering, as opposed to those that are discouraging and make us feel marginalized. We can choose to think of ways to overcome adversity, or we can choose to remain victims. I have chosen to persevere.

There are days when I'm reminded of the horrific abuse I've endured, yet I choose to get up each day and start fresh, thankful for all the good in my life. I am no longer afraid of the future. I fear the past repeating itself. I am haunted by the memories of those who have hurt me, yet I do not live my life in fear. That would rob me of time. The indulgences given to fear take away from our sense of hopefulness. So, I live in the now, with a view to what lies ahead.

HEART WARRIOR: TIME HELPS BUT LOVE HEALS
BY MARLA DAVID

I'm holding my heart in my left hand. My blood is pouring through my fingers. I look down and see it pooling on the floor, splatter marks surrounding it. I feel the warmth of it, smooth and thick; its dark and bright colours mixed together as the old and fresh blood meet. I look down to my chest. My heart has been removed from my body, and I'm unclear how it got out.

Breathe, Marla, breathe.

I take a deep breath in and swallow. I choke on my saliva, and then salty tears flow down across the bridge of my nose and onto my pillow. My hand comes up to my mouth and stifles a cry. It was a dream, after all; it didn't actually happen, despite how real it felt.

I reach towards my chest to feel my heart beating inside of me; my amygdala moves into fight or flight mode. *Breathe, Marla, Breathe.*

My heart has been ripped out of me many times throughout my life. I've mended it again and again, sewing the threads carefully; weaving them in and out. My heart is scarred and worn, but it beats strongly.

I found myself further and further from my home, and I
Guess I lost my way
There were oh-so-many roads
I was living to run and running to live

* * *

> *I began to find myself searching*
> *Searching for shelter again and again*
> *Against the wind*
> *A little something against the wind*
> *I found myself seeking shelter against the wind*
>
> — *Against the Wind, Bob Seger*

The storms of life affect us all. As an emotional and sensitive person (an empath), the storms of my life have taken an especially heavy toll. As Neil Young put it so beautifully, I've been *"searching for a heart of gold."* But I've come to believe that that heart of gold is my own—a heart which can endure this life adventure I'm on.

> *And the seasons they go round and round*
> *And the painted ponies go up and down*
> *We're captive on the carousel of time*
> *We can't return we can only look behind*
> *From where we came*
> *And go round and round and round*
> *In the circle game*
>
> — *The Circle Game, Joni Mitchell*

In my quest to evolve and better understand myself, I had to look deep within, addressing matters of the heart. It has been a raw journey thus far, as it definitely hurts to revisit my wounds. But uncovering and acknowledging the truths—my truths—has been one of the most freeing things I've ever experienced. I've been able to extinguish the power these truths once held over me, giving me a new perspective, and a new paradigm by which to live. This journey of personal growth has brought with it a treasure chest of riches for me, and I've learned there is a pattern to my life—the pattern of a broken heart.

I remember so vividly, the first time my heart was broken. It happened when I was but a wee girl. My Bubbie was a major role model in my life; she lived with us, and spent a lot of time with my sister and me. Bubbie was your typical European grandmother, with white hair, a large bosom, and she always wore a dress with an apron. I would lie on her bed cuddling with her while she told me stories and brushed my hair. She just had that nurturing way about her.

Life went on beautifully with Bubbie in our home. It was a constant, a certainty in my life. However, one day my Uncle Willy came over and told us that Bubbie would be going away. We were to go in to say our goodbyes. I didn't understand, but I did as I was told.

I went in quietly, so confused about why she was going away. Bubbie was very weak. She said never mind about that, and told me she would always love me. Bubbie gave me her little pillow, which I still have today.

That night she passed away. I had no concept of death at that age, so all I knew was that she was gone. It tore my heart out. Her loss was a void that I couldn't understand. To this day, there are times I grasp that pillow hard and cry into it, with a pain so deep.

Oh, the first cut is the deepest, baby I know
The first cut is the deepest
Try to love again
– The First Cut is the Deepest, Cat Stevens

Just as I was healing from losing my Bubbie, my heart was soon broken again. We moved from our home to the apartment building where my father's parents lived. This forced us to leave our butterscotch-coloured cat Blondie behind, the one we found in the neighbour's garbage bin. I had developed a close bond with the cat, and leaving it behind was devastating. On top of that, I would be losing my backyard. I loved that yard: the garden, the rose bush, the lawn, and the birthday parties. I was being removed from what I thought was paradise.

> *But my pretty countryside*
> *Had been paved down the middle*
> *By a government that had no pride*
> — *My City Was Gone, The Pretenders*

Despite living in the "brick box," I found ways to improvise. I went to the end of the street where there was a field, and I would run and try to catch grasshoppers. It was my space and I felt like nature's child, pure and free. I would collect dandelions and blow the seeds in the wind. I watched for butterflies, jar in hand. This was a short reprieve though, because the city expropriated the land for a future expressway. Nature has always been important to me. I loved being at summer camp, in the woods, and on the lake. Along with taking my field away, the city also tore down the apartment buildings. My best and only friend Rosemary and her cat, Snow White, were forced to move. Double whammy—another blow to my heart. I couldn't understand why things were constantly being taken away.

It was around this time that I learned I was adopted. I didn't really grasp the meaning of it, so I made no fuss about it. I did begin to feel as though I didn't fit in anywhere. "Belonging" was a word that didn't include me. It wasn't true, but I somehow convinced my mind to think that way. This was a limiting belief which stayed with me for most of my life, paving a negative path forward. I overheard my father's mother once say that *I wasn't of her blood.* Ouch. This cut directly into my heart. I just didn't know who I was. Although the pain was difficult to bear, eventually I learned to live within its confines.

In fifth grade, there was an incident that shaped my very existence, warping the way I perceived myself in relation to the external world. I came home from school to an empty apartment, so I just waited in the exterior hall for my mom. A couple of boys from the school, peers of mine, came into the building and ushered me down to the furnace room, where they exposed my privates. I was scared, vulnerable, and completely humiliated. The worst part of the whole event was, the boys told stories, untruths, and rumours got back to my parents. My dad asked to speak to me.

> *Tell me lies*
> *Tell me sweet little lies*
> *If I could turn the page*
> *In time then I'd rearrange just a day or two*
> *Close my, close my, close my eyes*
> – Little Lies, Fleetwood Mac

Feelings of shame and utter uselessness engulfed me as I stood before my dad, listening as he blamed *me*. It was as though I was responsible for what had happened, and I felt completely broken and unlovable. How could this have transpired? What did I do to bring this on? I must have really done something bad in life to have to endure the event, and the ostracizing that followed. The guilt was agonizing. Even through my high school years, whenever *those* boys would see me, they would make fun of me. I kept to my few friends and felt like a loser, an outsider. In hindsight, I see how this one event greatly shaped my life. I became more withdrawn and shy, had increased fears of life, and my self-worth was deteriorated.

This was difficult to break through and recover from, but my heart began to heal a bit as time went on.

I started to date, and eventually I married. This was an exciting time in my life. Past hurts were healing, and I finally felt like I belonged somewhere. After marrying, I had only one ambition: to become a mother. But this goal brought forth fresh heartache. I was not getting pregnant, and as I underwent test after test, I felt like a slab of meat. Eventually we decided upon adoption, but two times, the birth parents changed their minds after the babies were born. Twice my heart was torn from me.

Just when I could endure no more, I became pregnant. But I miscarried, and my dream moved further beyond reach. I felt totally useless as a woman. I couldn't even become a mother! God was punishing me, perhaps for what had happened in my past. Guilt raged through me and bad thoughts took reign. It was a dark time in my life.

> *Just like Pagliacci did*
> *I try to keep my sadness hid*
> *Smiling in the public eye*
> *But in my lonely room*
> *I cry the tears of a clown*
> *When there's no one around*
> *— The Tears of a Clown, Smokey Robinson*

I persevered with the drugs and tests, and another adoption came up. This time it came to fruition, and we became parents to a beautiful, healthy baby girl. I was concerned that the birth mother would change her mind, but after a week, the final call came, and there was jubilation in our home. I was a mother. My dream had finally come true. From such a low came the ultimate high. While I was enjoying being a first-time mom, I learned I was pregnant again. I was elated. I delivered a healthy baby girl, just seven months after my first daughter was born. My heart was full. And what's more, I got pregnant again! My third daughter was born just over two years later. I was in mommy heaven, enveloped in daily mommy life. Our family was close-knit. I was feeling the love, and love was healing my heart.

I put every effort into raising my family, and I grew as a person during this period. Parenthood taught me how to "be" in the world. I thank my daughters for being my biggest teachers in life. I wouldn't be the woman I am today without the validation of being a mother. My daughters taught me unconditional love—how to give it, and how to receive it. It is more profound to love when it is returned unconditionally.

During this time, I lost my Auntie Lilly, who was like another mother to me during my formative years. She reminded me of Bubbie, but Auntie Lilly never had children of her own. She'd had a hard life, and through her example I learned what it was like to have little, but give a lot. She embodied the kind of compassion I admired, and she loved my daughters and me. Auntie took ill and moved to long-term care, where she passed away. As I sat with her body, I closed her eyes, and recalled her saying that family members would come for her when it was her time. I knew she had gone to join them. My heart was heavy with grief as I mourned the life of the woman who had helped raise me.

Time can bring you down, time can bend your knees

Time can break your heart, have you begging please, begging please

Beyond the door there's peace I'm sure

And I know there'll be no more tears in heaven

– Tears in Heaven, Eric Clapton

When I turned forty, I became melancholy, as my marriage of almost twenty-five years was coming to an end. It was just something I sensed deep within me. I was caught up being a mommy for many years. But when the girls got older, I needed a different purpose in life. It wasn't so much the marriage, as it was a kind of restlessness within me—a feeling that there was just more out there. Time had changed my perspective, and I felt that I had been stagnating. There was no Marla in the equation anymore. I didn't feel I had a personal or individual identity other than that of a wife and mother. I needed to spread my wings. I felt incomplete; something was missing.

It took me seven years from this realization to have the guts to finally separate from my husband. I was worried about my girls, and in mourning over a marriage I thought would last forever. Fear took over my thoughts. I felt responsible for the break up of the marriage, because I was the one who initiated it. I knew this one act of mine would shift things in all our lives forever.

That fear manifested in the form of custody, as two of my children chose to live with their father. This was a devastating blow. I had no say in my daughters' lives, because I was not the custodial parent. How could this have happened when I was a stay-at-home mom? I was hurt, helpless, consumed by pain. I felt like an utter failure. I was fortunate to have a great support network of family and friends, but it was an achingly difficult time in my life.

Stop draggin' my,

Stop draggin' my,

Stop draggin' my heart around

There's people running 'round loose in the world

Ain't got nothing better to do

Than make a meal of some bright eyed kid

– Stop Draggin' My Heart Around, Tom Petty & Stevie Nicks

Many people told me that time would heal. It helped to ease some of the pain, but only through distraction. Events and a busy schedule kept my mind from thinking constant negative thoughts, but it always meandered back to the fear, guilt, shame, and my overall failure as a mother, wife, daughter, and person. Those negative aspects of my self-image were always there, even when hidden beneath a mask.

I tried hard to move on with my life. I stayed open-minded to see where this new life of mine would take me. I had a hard time dealing with the divorce, and I had to mourn the marriage at my own pace. But during this tumultuous time, I started dating and saw that there was a possibility of another chance at marriage. I viewed this as the portal to a new life, a new chapter, and perhaps something toward my destiny.

Two and a half years after separating, I was again under the chuppah, declaring my vows. I was generally happy, and I kept myself busy in my new life. My daughters were growing up and they were busy with their lives. We were all moving on.

In February of 2007, the first man I ever loved passed away. I spent my entire life seeking my father's approval; I adored him. Dad was smart, funny, and personable. He and Mom shared a lasting love. Dad was such a powerful force in my life, and I couldn't conceive of an end to his influence. His death catapulted me into a whole new universe of grief. Even though I had other people in my life, I felt alone. My rock, my stability in this crazy world was gone, and again I felt like my heart was torn from me. It has been ten years since his death, and I still struggle with my emotions. I visit his grave often.

I look at the world and notice it's turning

While my guitar gently weeps

With every mistake we must surely be learning

Still my guitar gently weeps

– While My Guitar Gently Weeps, Beatles

One February evening five years ago, everything came crashing down. I was feeling especially despondent, very vulnerable, and alone. My limiting beliefs and low self-esteem were unleashed and my mind was plagued with self-loathing. I was distraught beyond hope; I contemplated suicide. My heart had had enough. It was my dog who distracted me by walking into the room, which brought me back to my senses. I checked myself into the hospital. During the darkest hour of that night, with the police constable guarding the door, I had an epiphany. I knew there was an answer to my unhappiness. I had to find the "why" of my melancholy; I had to dig deep. I knew embarking on this journey was part of my destiny, so I embraced the darkness and began on my new path.

Hello darkness, my old friend
I've come to talk with you again
Because a vision softly creeping
Left its seeds while I was sleeping
And the vision that was planted in my brain
Still remains
Within the sound of silence
– The Sound of Silence, Simon & Garfunkel

As I read and took courses, I began to see my life in a new light. I plumbed the depths to find my "why," and that is how I learned that most of my problems were self-inflicted. Years of warped thoughts and poor memory, marred by attached and unchecked emotions, exacerbated my faulty belief system.

Upon acknowledging this, I began to make some changes in my life to support and compliment the authentic Marla.

Through meditation I have learned to be still, and in this stillness I have found peace and solace. I have let go of things that do not serve my purpose. Resentment, anger, and anything that does not support a peaceful existence have no place in my world. I am fortunate to have more clarity now, but it was hard-fought.

I recognized that during recent years, my soul had gone into hibernation. It was as though it detached from me, existing on the outside. I was Marla, but the *real* me was inaccessible. I had lost myself somewhere, becoming someone I didn't even recognize. Where were my values? How did I come to live with a skewed version of myself? I made the choice to separate from my second husband.

> *There's a fat old lady outside the saloon;*
>
> *laying out the credit cards she plays Fortune.*
>
> *The deck is uneven right from the start;*
>
> *all of their hands are playing apart*
>
> *– Farewell to Kings, Rush*

It's been seven months now, and my heart is heavy. I thought this would be "it," but I had been seeing my life through rose-coloured glasses. Going into the marriage, I still hadn't done the necessary work on myself. Almost twelve years in, I saw things with more clarity, and the marriage just wasn't what it seemed. I had a certain amount of trepidation going through divorce a second time. Anxiety has gripped me, as well as feelings of failure, and fear of being alone. At times, I feel my body swaying like I am on the subway, but the sensation is internal; I'm not actually moving. *Breathe, Marla, breathe.* I feel grateful that I take the time to meditate and breathe. I also have faith that going through divorce is exactly what I'm supposed to be doing. Huge lessons have been learned through this process, but why do the lessons have to hurt so much?

> *I learned the hard way*
> *That they all say things you want to hear*
> *And my heavy heart sinks deep down under you*
> *And your twisted words, your help just hurts*
> *You are not what I thought you were*
> *Head under water*
> *And they tell me to breathe easy for a while*
> *The breathing gets harder, even I know that*
>
> *– Love Song, Sara Bareilles*

Lately my mind is often on my mom, who is ninety-six years old and suffers from dementia. She is a shell of the woman she once was, which hurts my heart. I know she is not in pain, and I still have her presence, for now, in whatever condition she is in. This is her journey.

At the same time, Sunshine, my precious little RCA Victor dog, has passed over the rainbow bridge. She had been by my side for almost twenty devoted years. I did my best for her. I know it was her time, just like the rest of my fur babies. I could not allow her to suffer any longer. I spent her last afternoon comforting her, as she had done so often for me. Then I did the right thing for her: I let her go. I was with her as she took her last breath. This is the fourth dog I've lost in the span of six months. Last fall, my little Heinz 57 dog, Harley, lost control of her back end when her spine became severely compromised. Two days later, she was euthanized. I looked into her eyes, glassed over from the immense pain, and as the veterinarian inserted the last needle, I whispered into her ear that she was loved. Shortly thereafter, my dogs Buddy and Paws crossed the rainbow bridge together. I take solace in the dogs I still have, knowing that all creatures on earth have an allotted time, and one day it will be their turn as well. Reflecting on times like this, I can see how I have evolved.

With these new perspectives, I continue to uncover my soul's purpose. I question my very existence in this world. I have found Marla again; the pure soul who came into this life full of hope and dreams. There's still a long way to go, and it thrills me when I consider that, because I enjoy the essence of mystery. I challenge my fears these days. Without confronting them by stepping out of my comfort zone, I cannot grow. I've allowed love to thrive, and in doing that, my heart is growing; my capacity to love is ever greater. Like a river, my life energy is again flowing through me to the sea, to Source. I regularly utilise affirmations, meditation, and rituals, which have unlocked the key to serenity and peace in my life. I know life will throw things my way, but just like a duck in water, I will let it slide right off me. My heart may be ripped out again one day, but I'm ready to embrace the good and the bad. The difference now is, I've learned how to better handle the rocky times, and I have faith in the entire process. My daughters are also thriving, and I have much joy and contentment in that area of my life. I will soon be a grandmother. There is so much promise ahead. I am grateful for all the wonderful things in my life.

I used to fear that having my heart torn so often would cause it to harden. But greater than anything that has hurt me is the love in my heart and soul. Love has been the catalyst in my overcoming obstacles and challenges. Embracing the love inside of me has allowed me to carve out personal time to do those things which ignite my soul. I've learned to set healthy boundaries for myself, while continuing to shower love on those I cherish. I've learned forgiveness, and that has been a big step toward my healing. I healed from the inside out with love, and if I did it, anyone can! Most importantly, I still have my strong heart, firmly intact, albeit scarred. I've learned that *time helps, but it is love that ultimately heals*. I believe this unequivocally.

I couldn't have a vision for my best life until I could first define it. I needed to be precise about what I wanted in each area of my life. The rest is left to the Universe to figure out. As far as becoming the person I wanted to be, I first accepted myself, just as I am, with all my imperfections and flaws. I live each day striving toward love and the best version of myself. I am a **heart warrior**. There's nothing that can stop me from expressing my love in as many ways as I can. It is what I'm here for, and what I do best.

I can't recall last time I opened my eyes to see the world as beautiful

And I built a cage to hide in

I'm hiding, I'm trying to battle the night...

* * *

Let love conquer your mind

Warrior, warrior

Just reach out for the light

Warrior, warrior

* * *

I am a-yeah-yeah-yeah-yeah

Warrior, warrior of love!

– Warrior, Aurora

CHOOSING HAPPINESS
BY DEBBIE DOOLITTLE

From the age of two and a half until seven, my younger brother John and I slept together in the same bed. I would always sleep on the inside, closest to the wall so he could protect me from my nightmares. "Come on, John, it's time for bed. I'll get in first," I would say. And in I'd get.

My family lived in a trailer park in Newfield, New York, just ten miles outside of Ithaca. It was a clean, new trailer park, where most residents were young families trying to save money for a house, just like my parents were. With tons of other kids to play with in the neighbourhood, my brothers and I were never bored. Winters were long, cold, and snowy but our summers were warm and humid.

One particular summer, when I was two and a half years old, my uncle came to stay with us for a few weeks. We loved our uncle. He played with us, tickled us, and swung us around. We laughed and had the best time.

During my uncle's visit, my parents went out one day and left my brothers and me in his care. Why wouldn't they? We loved him and were happy to be with him—until he put us down for a nap that day. Our trailer was small so my brothers and I shared one bedroom with a bunk bed. Normally, I slept on the bottom, my older brother Bill slept on the top, and my youngest brother John was still in his crib. That day, my uncle put John down in the top bunk with Bill, and I remember thinking that wasn't the way it was supposed to be. Bill complained. With frustration in his voice, my uncle angrily told Bill to shut up and go to sleep. Like Dr. Jekyll and Mr. Hyde all of a sudden it was like he had flipped a switch and turned into a monster. That's when he molested me. I cried and cried. He yelled at me to stop crying so I put my thumb in my mouth to self-soothe and looked off towards a clock that was hanging on the wall. I felt as though I had emotionally left my body. My one saving grace was a voice I heard inside my head saying, "Never forget this because someday you will need to understand what happened."

Finally, he stopped.

The next day we all loaded into the family car to drop off my uncle at my other uncle's house about three hours away. I remember that trip like it was yesterday. My mother was upset with me because I wouldn't go to the bathroom the whole way there and the whole way home.

Shortly after that, my nightmares began and plagued me throughout my entire childhood. This was the reason my younger brother and I started sleeping in the same bed with me always on the inside against the wall. We slept this way until I was seven when my family moved into our first house where we each had our own bedroom. My nightmares would continue for years to come.

I remember thinking that I must have been a bad girl for my uncle to hurt me like that. Not knowing how to communicate my pain, I started taking out my emotions on my beloved dolls. They were my babies; normally, I loved my dolls more than anything. After my uncle hurt me, I would take my dolls' clothing off and spank them as if to punish them for bad behaviour. My mother was disturbed by this and as I would find out later, she and my father stopped spanking me when I didn't behave because they thought I was mimicking them.

Thankfully, my uncle never hurt me like that again. He would at times act inappropriately by hugging me too closely or by asking personal questions that made me uncomfortable. I had no choice but to forgive him at an early age. He was in my life. He was my father's brother. My parents didn't know the truth and wouldn't for a long time to come.

Life went on and my parents were finally able to move us out of the trailer park and into a house. We moved to the town of Newfield, New York, walking distance to my school and nearby shops. There was a bank, a post office, a library, three churches, and two little grocery stores. One of the stores had old-fashioned candy in jars behind a glass enclosure. As children, my brothers and I would press our little faces up against the glass to pick the penny candy we wanted. And if we were really lucky, sometimes the old storeowner would give us some for free. It was a neighbourhood full of kids running through the streets just like in the movies on Halloween and all of the parents knew each other.

My parents' relationship was a struggle, but as little kids we always felt they loved each other. Things changed when my parents decided to start a band with my "uncle." All of a sudden our house became party central with alcohol flowing out of every corner. My youngest brother, only nine years old at the time, would sneak beer from the keg. This phase was the catalyst for his eventual alcohol addiction, one that he would never recover from. During this phase, we would hear our parents' vicious fights while we were tucked quietly in our beds at night. One morning, we went downstairs and saw my mother with a black eye. To protect us from the truth, she lied and said she had run into the bathroom door by accident.

Our chaotic home life eventually led to my parents' separation. Their divorce left my younger brother devastated and traumatized. My older brother kept to himself, and I, on the other hand, only wanted my mother and father to be happy.

After their divorce, my mother started working three jobs to support us. She would get up at 4:00 AM, go to work, and come home after a few drinks at the local bar. In her absence, I was left to look after my younger brother. Looking back, I now realize that I felt a lot of pressure acting as a caregiver in my early teenage years. That's when things started to get bad for me. I felt detached from anything meaningful in my life so I would sneak out of the house to party looking for any connection I could find. My younger brothers' emotions, on the other hand, manifested in anger. On the verge of an eruption, my brother made the decision at fourteen to leave my mother and go live with my father, thinking things would be better for him. Meanwhile, my older brother managed to get his girlfriend pregnant and ended up married at the age of seventeen.

Devastated by my parents' divorce, I felt incredibly depressed and alone. During one of my particularly bad phases, my mother let me stay out of school for two weeks—that's how depressed I was. Through it all, my mother tried her best to be there for us but really didn't know what it meant to be a good parent. In desperate need of some guidance, she sought out a therapist for psychological support. But back then anxiety and depression was still very misunderstood, and unfortunately she didn't get the help and guidance she needed.

Likewise, my father had a difficult time coping with their divorce and stayed drunk for years to come. Their custody arrangement meant that I lived primarily with my mother and went to visit my father every other weekend. Unfortunately, his drinking made being with him uncomfortable. One time, when he was driving us home after a weekend visit, he took his hands off the wheel and wanted me to take it from him. I had no Idea how to drive or steer a car. To this day I don't know how we survived, but somehow we made it home okay.

Sometimes, to escape the dysfunction and madness, I would dream of a happier time in our lives when my parents were still together. We had a swing set and a big old tree we used to climb right outside our trailer. Without a care in the world I'd swing for hours. Every time I'd climb the tree I'd never be able to get down, so my older brother who was probably about six or seven would hold out his arms and tell me to jump. Too afraid, I would scream like a damsel in distress until my father would come running to save me. My dad has always been and still is my hero, for he too has endured a lot in his life.

My father came from a large family of nine siblings. My grandfather was a child molester and molested most, if not all, of his children. Unfortunately my father was no exception. In spite of this fact, my father still maintained a relationship with his parents. During one of our visits I remember my grandfather playing with us and my mother coming to get me, telling me not to get too close to him because he was a "dirty old man." Looking back, she clearly knew the type of monster he was. I didn't understand what she meant at the time, but I later found out that my aunt Dotty, my father's younger sister, committed suicide at the age of sixteen. I suspect his own daughter had been one of his victims. As a child, I paid close attention, gathering bits and pieces of information, storing them away in my memory bank in hopes I would fit it all together one day. And I did. The pieces started to make sense as I grew older and came to understand that unfortunately, I wasn't the only one who sustained sexual abuse in my family and that I wasn't my uncle's only victim.

Coming from such a large extended family, I had many cousins all close in age. One day my cousin Barb confided in us that she had been abused by the same uncle that abused me. She said he had held a knife to her throat and told her he would kill her if she told anyone. Well, she did tell, and her mother accused her of lying. I don't know for certain why her mother would deny her daughter's story, although I suspect she had been a victim of abuse herself. Supporting her daughter's story would mean having to come forward, which I don't think she was ready to do. Family denial was the biggest battle we faced and it didn't stop with Barb's mother.

Years later, as adults, three of us cousins stood up and spoke out to stop the family abuse and incest by reporting my abusive uncle to the police after we had found out that he had been accused of molesting his five-year-old granddaughter. My uncle tried to deny the allegations. The little girl was bipolar and he used that as a defense strategy. Unfortunately, it worked in his favour and although my uncle was investigated, he was never convicted. My cousin, the girl's father supported my uncle in his defense. He really wanted to believe that his father couldn't have done this to his daughter. The whole thing was out of our hands. I checked in with the police department a few times but I wasn't able to obtain any information. My cousins and I felt defeated. We were unable to protect this little girl from her sexually abusive grandfather, but I had warned my cousin years earlier to keep his daughter away from him.

Eventually we found out that child protective services got involved and ended up removing the little girl from her home about two years after her accusations. To make matters worse, my two female cousins that stood up with me didn't end up receiving the love and support by their parents that one would expect when admitting to having been a victim of sexual abuse. Instead, both of their mothers didn't want to believe them and denied everything. My parents, on the other hand were far more supportive and by comparison, I considered myself lucky. Although my cousins and I felt powerless in convicting my uncle, collectively we had had the power to finally let the truth be known. Our extended families knew we were no longer willing to stay silent and a rift had formed between them. Our efforts had not been for nothing.

I don't know where I'd be today if it weren't for the love and support my parents gave when I finally told my mother at age twenty-six what had happened to me so many years prior. I was going through my first divorce and seeing a counsellor. In order to heal and let go of the pain, my therapist encouraged me to be honest with my parents. With all of the strength I could muster, I faced the truth and told them. As heartbreaking as it was for them to hear, and equally as painful as it was for me to say, it was an important step on my road to recovery and a necessary one if I wanted to live a life with my soul intact. My spirit had been broken and I needed to fix it.

After I was done talking, my mother corroborated my entire story. She remembered the day it happened, my uncle running down the hall zipping up his pants. At the time, she told my father to have a talk with him. My father threatened that if he ever touched me, he would kill him. The next day they took him back to stay with my other uncle, just as a precaution. They didn't know for sure what had happened until the day I told them. My mom remembers the exact year. It was summertime and my birthday is in December so we knew I must have been two and a half, exactly how I remembered it.

The relief I felt was like no other. Not only did I feel relieved, but I also felt extremely grateful. I distinctly remember feeling so lucky for having the love and support of parents who believed me. It was a love I never questioned, ever. Although I felt as though a weight had been lifted by telling my parents, I couldn't help but feel very sad for my cousins and couldn't imagine how it must have felt to be called a liar by their own parents.

The same voice I had heard the day my uncle molested me repeated itself over and over again throughout the years, "Don't ever forget this, for someday, you will need to understand." I didn't know where the voice originally came from, but I knew it didn't come from me. As I grew older I started to wonder. Was it me from the future? Was it an angel? Was it a spiritual guide? Was it God? I still don't know for sure, but I am and always have been grateful for that voice.

As you could imagine, having a name like Debbie Doolittle didn't make growing up very easy. Not only would kids bully me in school, I also had undiagnosed dyslexia, which made learning how to read and write challenging, to say the least. Many days I would just cry because my bullies were validating my own thoughts that I was dumb. This, along with my very low self-esteem from my earlier abuse, led me to wonder what was wrong with me and I was therefore very shy. I wasn't athletic either so I was always the last one to be picked for team sports. No one wanted me on their team. The year of my parents' divorce was the year I learned to fight back and stand up for myself. I was being teased about my last name and I finally said, "Yes, I can clearly talk to animals because I can talk to you." Needless to say, I was never teased about my name again.

My one saving grace while in high school during my senior year was a teacher who finally recognized I needed words of encouragement and how powerful it can be to have someone believe in you. He said, "Debbie, you are intelligent. Go look up the meaning." And I did. Intelligent means to have the ability to learn. Well, I can learn! I may not be able to spell very well or read very fast, but I can learn! His encouragement is what eventually led me to try harder in school and pursue a career in hairdressing.

Self-taught at age fourteen, I realized my passion. I got out the sewing shears and started cutting my friends and even my brother's hair for practice! I would beg just about anyone to let me cut their hair. It's what kept me in school since I knew I had to pass my grades in order to go to cosmetology in eleventh grade. Making women feel beautiful and special was something I wanted to do more than anything. In my heart I knew it would be my path to a happy and fulfilled life. Although I needed to finish school to make that dream a reality, I needed to learn a few more important life lessons first. That's when Paul came around.

I met my first husband Paul when I was sixteen years old. He was a year ahead of me in school and had gorgeous dark blond hair and blue eyes. Our relationship offered me a sense of security from the madness of my dysfunctional home life. Paul was also from a broken home, and while his family was falling apart and moving away, he chose to stay close by and live with his grandmother so he could be close to me.

Paul's grandmother was a traditional woman with a generous heart. Her rules made it difficult for us to see each other, but we would find ways. When I turned eighteen I'd had enough of living at home and I wanted to go live with Paul at his grandmother's house. We were in love. I felt the most secure with Paul and wanted to be with him always. His grandmother insisted we get married if we were to live together, so we did. Given my age and that I still had another year of high school left to complete, my mother was furious and tried to talk me out of it. As it turns out, my mother's instincts were right.

As I got to know more about Paul's family, I learned that his wasn't much different than my father's growing up: Paul's father hated women and had been abusive to Paul's mother.

Although Paul never physically hurt me, he instinctively thought he should be able to control me, especially where money was concerned. Paul was always taking my money without asking or offering to pay me back. One day, his cousin gave me five dollars to give to Paul, money that he had borrowed. I wasn't working at the time so I could focus on finishing cosmetology school and didn't have any money of my own. I took the five dollars and bought a razor and pantyhose. When he discovered what I had done, he yelled at me and told me never to take his money again. In that moment, I promised myself that I would never be without my own money and I would never depend on anyone to take care of me again.

Fed up with my husband's controlling nature, but not knowing how to escape, suicidal thoughts invaded my mind and I stopped eating. I knew something needed to change. That was the beginning of the end—the end of my first marriage but also the end of my selfish thoughts. In my heart of hearts, committing suicide wasn't an option. I couldn't leave my nephews, nieces, and siblings to feel the way I did when I lost my aunt Dottie. No doubt Dottie suffered at the hands of my grandfather just as the others had, but nonetheless, she was ultimately my saving grace. I used to think that she was so selfish by taking her own life because it meant I would never get the chance to know her. She was beautiful, popular in school, and sweet. Everyone loved her. Her sacrifice taught me the ultimate lesson and is what gave me the strength and foresight to stay alive. It was time to seek counselling.

Listening to the lyrics of Michael Jackson's "Man in the Mirror" back in 1987, Whitney Houston's "Greatest Love of All," and Bette Midler's "The Rose" gave me the sense of empowerment I needed to survive my darkest time. As a starting point, my therapist gave me self-help books to kick start my journey such as *The Road Less Traveled* by M. Scott Peck. Throughout my healing process I would look at others around me who were happy and successful and wondered what it was about them and how they had achieved it. Instead of choosing to be devastated and immobilized by my past or the downfall of my marriage, I eventually, with a lot of hard work, chose to use other people's success as my own motivation. Instead of saying, "Why them, and why not me?" I allowed those achieving stability and happiness to give me hope and resolve. I've come to realize happiness is a choice. It's really that simple.

It took me ten long years to realize Paul and I were no longer meant to be together. Choosing to divorce was a devastating decision and we struggled for two years before finally releasing each other. I loved Paul but knew I couldn't be with him anymore. Our marriage was too toxic. Paul and I finalized our divorce in 1991, exactly ten years to the day from when we were married. After it was over, I refocused my energy and continued putting my cosmetology license to good use. In spite of it all, I was still able to maintain my focus and passion for the beauty industry. No one was going to hold me back.

While married, I had been renting a booth in a salon. This experience allowed me to quickly learn the industry, but it also gave me the confidence to know that I had the necessary tools to make it as an entrepreneur. By 1993, after seven years of renting a booth, I opened my own salon, began hiring employees, and created an environment for them to make a living and engage in personal development. Twenty-three years and many awards later, I'm now a successful salon and spa owner. Unfortunately, the journey towards my professional success was still tainted with personal struggle.

After a second failed marriage, I couldn't figure out why I was repeating many of the same mistakes. My second divorce left me with familiar emotional pain and I was tired of feeling like I never had my own voice. Yearning to find myself, I knew there was something that was still missing. I felt stuck and scared that I would keep making the same mistakes so I chose to go for one-on-one spiritual life coaching. I didn't want to be a victim anymore once I realized that being a victim was my downfall. My coach taught me to trust myself and not take things personally. My perception of being repeatedly mistreated my entire life started to shift when I realized that it wasn't about me at all. My uncle didn't abuse me because he wanted to hurt me; he did it because he was hurting. My perpetrators were living inside their own story. Once I came to this realization, I was able to release myself from their stronghold and not take on their abuse as my own. After years of victimizing myself, I was finally able to choose happiness. With every painful event I've endured, I've been able to learn from it and evaluate how to move forward in order to ensure history did not repeat itself. Choosing to be happy instead of a victim was by far my best move yet. And without a doubt, I know I made the right decision.

LOVE IS LARGER THAN LOSS
BY CHRISTIE ECHEVERRI

My father fell and broke his tibia today. He was taking the garbage out and slipped on a patch of ice. After hearing this news, I thought to myself, *I should call Mom and make sure she knows.* Which is silly, because my mother has been dead for the better part of a year now. I still have those stomach-lurching pauses of recognition, though, moments that would seem halfway amusing if this were a gallows-humor sitcom, rather than genuine Life Without Mom. Occasionally I'll feel the split-second urge to call her, before my brain uploads the equivalent of a *404 nothing to be found here* page. Among her noteworthy qualities was my mother's gift for gab. Our weekend calls could easily surpass two or three hours—we'd say goodbye multiple times, only to launch into another topic. Chinese by birth but raised primarily in Brazil, my mother was an excellent conversationalist in any of the three languages she spoke.

One of the last things we discussed was Superbowl 50. She was rooting for the Broncos because of her fondness for the underdog and her respect for Peyton Manning. Mom was so weak that she couldn't stand unassisted, but in those few moments, discussing an interest we had long shared, I saw her again...the woman who would yell, "C'mon, rebound! REBOUND!" at the TV as our hometown Blazers blew another lead. I saw the person who would call me after every big game my teams played, win or lose. I saw my faithful friend, my tireless advocate; the woman who impressed so many with her strength, conviction, and award-winning cornbread.

As a child, I adored her existence. Last year I found a yellowed piece of notebook paper filled with hearts and stars. *Mommy you are cute you do so many things for me. I love you so much I am brocin wen you are not here.* She kept it all, every single scrap of my grammatically unsound ramblings. Mom taught me how to write cursive, and how to sew a pillowcase (I was actually thirty-six when the latter occurred). During the Color Me Beautiful craze of the '80s, she showed me what shades flattered my skin tone, and I stay away from yellow to this day. Unabashedly frugal, she taught me that, for an introvert like me, brokering a bargain wasn't over until I felt *very* uncomfortable. One of our favorite little games was "guess how much I paid?" If bargain hunting is a sport, I'm at least semi-pro now.

Perhaps the last thing she taught me was that I was strong enough to let her go.

We found out that Mom had breast cancer the same day I became a mother. Life can be meticulous and heartbreaking in its timing. The news was unexpected, but her prognosis was generally favorable. A lumpectomy was scheduled, and she came to Hawaii as planned to meet her ninth grandchild. I remember her holding Alex in the crook of her left arm while intently watching the Food Network, pen poised. She did this for hours, encouraging me to rest upstairs. Her shorthand was impeccable; after she died we found untold numbers of spiral notebooks filled with recipes, quotes, advice, and general miscellany.

Mom shared her strength and her knowledge freely, but loved learning from others. She possessed an acute sense of justice that, when insulted, ignited a fire. She had a tendency to hoard both the tangible—paper, folding chairs, bread from restaurants—and the intangible—eclectic wisdom, child-like wonder, compassionate feelings toward those less fortunate. She had the biggest heart of anyone I've ever known, which left her vulnerable, yet uniquely empowered to do good.

And oh, how she excelled at doing good. Motherhood is a sort of performance in the public arena of open judgment, an instinctive dance of self vs. seed. By that, I mean (many) women feel a requisite need to wholly submit to the needs of their children, particularly when they are young. We seek balance between motherhood and personhood, but consequently see both areas suffer. I don't think my mother experienced such internal conundrum—that pressing need to maintain one's pre-children identity. She was too busy fulfilling her life's purpose. I don't say that flippantly. Mom undoubtedly changed lives for the better, lives beyond the six she co-created.

About a year before she passed away, when she still had stamina that matched her sturdy convictions, Mom organized a fundraising dinner benefitting the people of Madagascar. She cooked with gusto, preparing traditional Malagasy food despite having no prior knowledge of it. She was like that, always—diving in to a cause headfirst, seeing opportunity where others saw obstacles. I am not my mother's daughter in this regard. I often feel aimless, adrift in a sea of both possibilities and limitations. While my worldview unfolds in shades of grey, Mom's outlook was black and white, right vs. wrong. She knew exactly what she was put on this earth to do, and had little patience for a neurotic list of figurative pros and cons. Who has time to doubt their abilities when the suffering of the world demands immediate action? She was a voice for the voiceless, a charming, cheerful, lovable force of nature. Mom shined when she served; her humor and utter lack of pretense drew others to her. I'm a splendidly flawed individual, but I like to think that I embrace the latter qualities on some level. My mother's influence runs deep; she had nary a disingenuous bone in her body.

I know I am not the woman my mother was. I carry her DNA, but I've never truly felt that I represented the best of her, the traits one hopes to keep alive through subsequent generations. She was the least vain person I've ever known, eschewing makeup after her third child. She rarely doubted herself, and didn't tend to ruminate or regret. Contrast that with my love of all things girly, and my maddening tendency to fold inward, flogging myself for the imperfections that only make me human. Mom was a genuinely happy person, whereas I have struggled with depression—at times severe—since my mid-teens. It took us years to reach a point of understanding, for my surly emo-like tendencies to be recognized as an illness rather than protracted apathy. But during some of my worst adult breakdowns, my mother was a lifeline, a haven in the tempest.

Thinking back to my teens, when quarrels were a daily occurrence facilitated by the slightest of perceived transgressions, I used to marvel at the idea that *this woman* birthed me. What did we have in common, who was she anyway? When I was ready to shed my selfish skin and listen, I learned who she was. Mom was the youngest of five children. She had a gift for reading people and anticipating needs. She ate rather noisily, as is customary for her culture. She made my father happy. She had an infectious laugh, a giggle that is dearly missed. She would have given her life for those she loved, and maybe even those she didn't. She would never let a guest go hungry. She had the heart of a warrior.

When I had matured enough to appreciate both her sacrifices and our differences, I decided we could best seal our newfound buddy status with a trip to Asia. It was my dream to see China with Mom. Although she initially balked at the idea (*"it's dirty, and the food isn't even that good!"*), in 2004 we touched down in Beijing. I felt giddy with the recognition of my roots. I had always been half-white, my father's daughter; now I belonged to my mother as well. At night, after full days of walking, gawking, and haggling, she would tell me stories about her ancestry. We came home with an abundance of stories ourselves, and I will treasure them always. Years later we would laugh over the "duck head incident," which occurred at a restaurant outside the Forbidden City. I had ordered Peking Duck soup, figuring a bowl of liquid was a good entry point for cuisine that featured innards and gizzards. A few benign spoonfuls later, the duck's severed head came wafting to the surface like some sort of vegan horror story. She nonchalantly finished the bowl for me while I hesitantly filled up on rice.

Mom is past tense now. She *was* confident, *was* happy, *loved* Jane Austen books and BBC miniseries, *championed* her children. I wish my boys had known her as she truly was—feisty, friendly, driven by a mission much larger than herself.

You've missed so much.

You're missed so much.

This winter has been prolifically wet (even by Portland standards), resulting in damp clothes, a dampened soul, and perpetual wet dog smell throughout our house. But yesterday the sun appeared against a blue, cloudless sky, where it stayed unhindered from dawn to dusk. Startled neighbors emerged from their homes, exposing pale limbs toward this welcome orb in the sky. I took my son to three different parks, all similarly packed with gleeful children. It was the kind of heart-swelling day that made me feel glad to be alive. But late that afternoon, as I stood in my kitchen doing nothing in particular, I felt the familiar lump of grief rise in my throat. *Mom's missing this. Mom will never again feel the sun on a cloudless day.* Sometimes, it is in joyful, contented moments that I miss her most.

She began dying when the falls started. I can only say this in retrospect; I suppose I was expecting some sort of official word that she had transitioned into the gloaming, with the next stop being permanent night. The fall that led my sisters and I to pack our bags occurred the second week of February. Mom had been admitted to the ER due to her incoherence as much as anything else. My father didn't want us to come down until she had a conclusive prognosis. We were all new at this, you see; the only person who'd witnessed a close relative dying was Mom herself, and her current lucidity varied from moment to moment. While I understood Dad's caution, I wasn't keen on waiting things out. I was the oldest daughter, which hardly gave me diagnostic superpowers, but did make me feel a strong sense of duty.

She didn't initially know who I was. I'd last seen her at Christmas, and now she looked as though she'd aged twenty years. Her face was swollen and sunken at the same time; the light in her eyes was noticeably absent. Her beautiful, black Asian hair—stick straight until menopause or some hormonal havoc rerouted its appearance—had been reduced to a few desolate clumps on her head. My sister and I took a moment in the hallway, digesting the awful truth about her current state. Was I in denial? Didn't I realize this was the end? I continued living my hopeful version of reality, sleeping on the floor of the nursing facility in case there was a positive development. Back at home, I changed her sheets in anticipation of her being discharged. Even if it was to die, I hoped she'd come home.

She never did. Mom slipped into a coma before passing away in Folsom, California on February 27, 2016. We buried her in the Sacramento Valley National Cemetery. Mom had been excited—yes, she really had—to discover she could be buried there, since it was low-cost. She had us laughing when levity was sorely needed.

After I received word of her passing, I immediately looked at the sky (or, rather, the ceiling), asking aloud, "Where have you gone, Mom?" Tears rolled down my cheeks, but intermingled with my grief was genuine confusion. *Where are you?*

My mother prepared letters for all of us, even as her handwriting became shaky and her memory, less sharp. In her four-page letter to me, she incisively catalogued my better qualities, the way only a person who's known you your whole life can. Mom did her best to build me up, knowing I would need all my strength in the heartrending days ahead. She also talked about temporary separation, and her resolute belief that she'd see us again on the other side. How I wish I could choose to latch onto this idea. For a sensitive sap, having my rational side hold court has been a surprising development. I don't know. If I had to address this with my boys—and someday, probably soon, I will—I'd say, no matter how painful loss is, boys, I can't state that I share her truths. You'll come to know your own soul, and maybe you'll align yourselves with Grandma's beliefs. I want to launch platitudes into the sky, comforting missives about a reunion someday. I want to tell you that she's looking over us, and after us. I want to believe in a force stronger than death.

But I just don't know.

For weeks after she passed away, I had trouble remembering her as she had actually been my first thirty-one years of life, before cancer struck. Mental images of my mother smiling, giggling, and engaging with friends and strangers alike were instead replaced by pictures of her sickly, disoriented, and physically unrecognizable. Her suffering was over, but that didn't stop me from reliving her final days, those days in which not even her dignity remained. So much chemo, so much pain... After six years spent battling cancer, she had been liberated. Still, I retained my helpless, panicky, *what's next* feelings, not knowing how to channel them. To release them entirely would be to acknowledge my new, motherless normal. *No, thank you*, I thought. *I'd rather wear this proverbial, weighted blanket a bit longer.* Sure, it was unnecessary, but I needed the familiarity, just until I could stop crying in the shower.

I've only dreamt about my mother once or twice. The first time, she was young and smiley, wearing a floral polyester dress with vibrant colors. I knew that dress from hours spent combing through our family photo drawer. She walked by me on the street, and my heart leapt into my throat. "Mom, MOM! It's me, it's Christie!" She turned around, still smiling. "Oh, I'm sorry...I don't know who you are?" Pitifully, or perhaps mercifully, that's where my recollection ends.

Somehow I thought that because I'd grown in her womb, heard her heartbeat from the inside—somehow I thought that I'd feel her presence after she was gone, the way people do in movies. In "movie loss," you get a gust of wind that blows a certain kind of leaf in your lap, reminding you of a childhood memory, her favorite tree—something poignant. In movie loss, grief is linear, progressively headed towards a place of healing.

In actuality, my grief is more a slow, zigzagging reconciliation between my heart and my mind. In the beginning, I couldn't remember a time when Mom wasn't the sun our family orbited around. Now, a year later, I struggle to remember when she was. It's been four seasons, full of holidays, firsts, new life. I marked a birthday the month after she died, and it felt like a parenthetical event without the preceding context. One could argue that death is the most natural thing in the world, but it was unnerving to "celebrate" a day we could no longer share.

The sound of her shuffling feet, strangely, is what I miss. Mom had a particular shuffle—akin to a flat-footed slipper devotee—but she was actually neither of those things. I used to be on alert for that shuffle, ready to stash away the contraband magazines I pored over, or formulate pleasing answers for an inquisition about school. In recent years, when I'd come to visit, the shuffle was stalwart and reliable, but no longer a harbinger of unease. We were friends, cohorts; it's a beautiful transition for your mother to become your bestie, especially after years spent thinking of her as a giant buzzkill dressed in church clothes.

So, Mom would shuffle around the kitchen, the sounds as familiar as the old pink nightgown she wore. *Putter putter putter*; dishes would clang and the faucet would run. *Shuffle shuffle clang shuffle.* You know how it's been estimated that people spend, like, three years of their life on the toilet? Well, following that model, I'd guess that Mom exhausted around seventeen years thinking or talking about food, meal planning, cooking, or grocery shopping. The kitchen was her domain, and for me the shuffle represented normalcy and comfort. When she stopped cooking and the sound all but ceased, a prominent hue from her colorful personality faded away.

I wasn't there when her spirit left her body, and I never said a Hollywood goodbye. I didn't sit by her bed and wait for my turn to clasp her hands, tearfully recalling four decades of memories. Instead I was at home in Portland, with my two young sons. I'd thought our whole family would gather 'round at the end, having had plenty of time to assemble from various corners of the country. It wasn't to be; Mom had her own timeline. But there is this: The last time I heard her voice, we chatted briefly, before she told me she loved me, and I responded in kind. There was nothing left unsaid between us— no latent apologies for regrettable teenage behavior (I addressed my remorse through bad Mother's Day poems she'd hang on the fridge), or disappointment that we'd put off a mother-daughter trip to Asia (check! There are numerous pictures of us trekking along the Great Wall). For a long-winded pair of opposites, having nothing left unsaid is a pretty substantial gift.

I think she'd agree, wherever she is.

LOVE BOOMERANG
BY ANGIE FIX

On a very cold, blistery day, my dear friend was driving me home from a chemo appointment. We started conversing about my chapter for this book, and I told her that I was still struggling with a topic choice. "Angie," said my wise friend, "if this were your last day on earth, what message would you want to deliver to the world?" Without hesitation I replied, "I would like to share with the world the power of love—its ability to heal, liberate, and make lives better. It's the miracle drug for all afflictions."

Having been diagnosed with breast cancer, this was more than lip service; I was facing my own mortality. In my heart, not my head, the message was screaming to get out. Why? Quite simply, because I have seen love work its magic time and time again. As I write this I am teary-eyed and have goosebumps all over my body. It's my soul's way of letting me know that I'm on the right path.

In my thirties, I had an epiphany about my childhood. I realized that I'd never wholeheartedly been loved. Early in life, my purpose had been clearly defined, and that was to be the caretaker of the family. I began to realize how I'd overextended myself in every aspect of my life to gain approval and a sense of belonging. Once I understood this, I had feelings of anger, deceit, unworthiness, and shame. *What was wrong with me? What had I done to deserve this treatment?* I didn't have answers and there was nowhere I could turn to get them. I felt I wasn't good enough to be loved unconditionally, a realization so painful that I formed a tough shield around me. Subconsciously, I had decided I was no longer going to let anyone hurt me—never again!

Superficiality became part of my character as my heart continued to shut down. I faked through a lot in my life, becoming a great pretender. Life was good as long as I didn't have to deal with the touchy-feely stuff. I also became very focused on me, which was a self-defense mechanism. I had to protect myself, so I adopted the mindset that it was either my way or the highway. I lived this way for many years, but there was always a feeling of anxiety, a longing for something deeper. In short, I never felt whole. A few years later, that all changed when life began to throw curveballs at my family. Tragedy followed tragedy, with no discernible end in sight. All that I knew was falling apart during this painful and confusing time.

What I didn't know then, is that the unravelling of my old pretentious life would become the birth of my new, meaningful life. I was about to discover the true power of love.

Material things that identified me no longer existed. I was being stripped of all external objects, which forced me to face the naked truth. I slowly began to comprehend that I had nothing but love to depend on. This was a foreign concept to me. Although I had loved in those plastic years, I now know I hadn't truly loved. Eventually, my focus shifted from what I was going to buy next, to how I was going to survive with my family. This is where I discovered the true joy and beauty of my children. They had so much to offer me which I had previously been blind to. Their innocence, resilience, and unconditional love started filling my every vessel. I was in awe of how wonderful that felt. My heart began expanding and feeling the love from them, which I returned, full force. For the first time in years I felt whole because I was rediscovering love. When I began to feel safe and comfortable with my children's love, I decided to open my heart wider to others. I was becoming less guarded and it was liberating. I thought to myself, *it can't get any worse than this ... what do I have to lose? Why don't I just be myself? Life is already pushing me in that direction.*

I no longer wished to be part of the herd. I wanted to evolve into who I was meant to be.

It wasn't easy, though. I had to re-identify myself not by what I had, but through discovering my true essence. I had to part with the social norms and pressures, and have the courage to stand up and follow my path. Compassion began to peek through my heart. I had always cared for others, but it was just that—cared, not loved. Keeping everyone at arm's length was safe. Having endured some pretty challenging times, I'd begun to have a deeper understanding of the human condition. It gave me profound insight into what people experience and I wanted to do my part to help as many people as I could. With that whisper in my heart, I coordinated several "homeless runs." My objective was not just to deliver clothing and nutritious food to the disadvantaged, but to do so while honouring their dignity. I disliked the idea of prepackaging food in brown bags. This was impersonal, and didn't offer choice. So, I decided to create a store-like environment in the back of my truck. My helpers and I would set it up in such a fashion that when our friends came by, they were able to select what they wanted. The look on their faces was priceless, as having choices was outside their norm.

My favourite part of our trips was engaging in conversation with them. Their stories furthered my compassion as I began to realize that homelessness is rarely a choice. There are always contributing factors such as mental health issues, addictions, and poor home lives. During our visits, many would hug me. Now trust me, they weren't at their best as far as personal hygiene was concerned, but this didn't bother me—I was exchanging a tender moment of love with them. By nature I am a bit of a germaphobe, so my lack of concern was surprising. Something inside me was shifting ... it was no longer about me!

As time went on, my passion for the homeless population grew deeper. There were ample opportunities to support them, particularly when I worked downtown. I wasn't selective about who to help because my heart always led me to the right people. On many occasions, I would just sit and talk to them. My friends thought I was crazy, but I never paid attention to them because I feel that when you do something from the heart, you will be protected. These people may have been cast aside by society, but they, too, deserved love and compassion.

One day on my way to the train station I met a young man who was begging on the street corner. People just walked by him with no eye contact, no acknowledgement. They were practically stepping on him! My heart pulled me in his direction. I sat on the sidewalk and we began to talk, all the while getting very strange looks from passersby. His name was Kevin and he began to tell me about his traumatic childhood. Both parents were addicts, the better of the two being his dad, who'd died when Kevin was only twelve. His mother had no use for him and was very abusive and negligent. He left home at a very early age and continued the cycle because he didn't know a better way. Kevin had been on the streets for a few years, and his face showed the trauma he'd suffered. He had a criminal record, and was not proud of his past, but he'd survived. A bit older now, Kevin was coming to the realization that he wanted a better life, but didn't know where to start. He had no support, no lifeline. To top it all off, his girlfriend had just given birth to a daughter, who was born disabled. Wow, I wondered—could this get any worse?

I asked Kevin to meet me the next day. With the help of several people I was able to gather some clothing, shoes, gift cards for food, and most importantly, information on how to acquire housing and employment assistance. It all fell into place in less than 24 hours. I was awestruck, but not surprised, because I've learned that when you reach out with your full heart, the universe conspires to make it happen. It uses us as tools to serve humankind. I met Kevin the next day and delivered all the information and goods to him. His eyes lit up like a Christmas tree. He said he would save the best clothing and shoes for when he went to visit his daughter at the hospital. He wanted to look his best for her, he wanted her to be proud of him. Those words brought tears to my eyes.

Many look at the homeless as a disposable part of our society, but they have feelings and dreams just like the rest of us. I explained to Kevin that several people should be credited for this. He was so grateful and in total amazement that people cared enough to help him. He asked me why I had stopped that day to talk to him. After all, I was a stranger, and his own mother had never shown any regard for him. My answer was, why not? I truly feel our job on earth is to help as many people as we can. This is what love looks like. It doesn't have to be conventional in perception or practice.

I met Kevin a few days later. He told me that he'd contacted the appropriate agencies and was in the process of acquiring housing and employment. My heart sang with joy as I walked to catch my train. It really does take a village to change a life.

As I began to recognize the value of love more deeply, it became apparent to me that it was like a boomerang. The more unconditional love I put out there, the more came back to me. Acts of kindness and love don't have to be big. They can be as simple as calling someone, buying a coffee, or offering a smile and a warm hug. These things make such an enormous difference in people's lives. Small gestures can turn a bad day into one of hope and comfort. Love is fluid, like a river. No matter what obstacles it faces it will find a way around.

A great little story to illustrate the power of love comes to mind. My husband has a prodigious green thumb and a great love for plants. Many years ago, before leaving town, he asked me to care for the plants with a specific regimen. I wasn't too keen on this—*oh brother, I have to take care of these things I don't even like, that occupy unnecessary space in my home.* Still, I followed the instructions to a T. Despite my diligence though, the plants were drooping and looked like they may die. I couldn't understand what I was doing wrong. My husband was quite surprised at their condition when he returned. I told him I'd done everything he had asked me to do. This may sound crazy, but within two days of his return the plants were perky and had returned to normal. Why, you may ask? The answer is quite simple—he offered them love by touching them and talking to them. Every living being flourishes when the energy of love is transmitted. My husband made a believer out of me and from that day forward, I had absolute respect for plant life. But my examples don't stop there.

I have worked in healthcare for close to thirty-five years. I can honestly say it has made me a better human being because every day I am given opportunities to make a difference in someone's life. When you are ill and incapacitated, all you want is for someone to treat you with love and respect. I repeatedly witness how patients with strong family support are happier and regain their health faster. On the other end of the spectrum, people who don't feel loved or supported, deteriorate very quickly. This is also evident in neonatal units. Babies who are born ill, premature, or drug-addicted thrive much more when they are held, cuddled and sang to. Human contact and love is critical in expediting their development and good health.

I have personally experienced the benefits of compassionate healthcare while undergoing treatment for cancer. The kinder the practitioners are, the easier my journey becomes. To demonstrate the opposite, one unpleasant appointment comes to mind. Treatment involves a lot of unpleasant poking and prodding. On this particular day, when I went to the lab to have blood work done I was received by a nurse who had a very sour look on her face. Her dialogue was even worse. Angrily, she said, "sit over there and put your arm out." As I sat down I thought, *wow, someone's having a bad day.* I guess everyone is allowed, but boy, I could feel the harsh energy emanating from her. Normally, having blood work done is not a problem, but when she started the procedure I felt a lot pain. It was as though she was ramming the needle into my arm. I breathed through it, knowing I've experienced worse lately—but never had a blood draw hurt as much as this. What was the difference? This nurse did not carry out her duties with love and compassion. Instead, she was angry, and it showed in her work.

I believe in the law of karma, which has become evident throughout my journey with cancer. The compassion and love I've strived to put forth, is now being returned to me. While delivering care, I did not foresee one day becoming a recipient—I operated the way I did because my heart was full of love and compassion. Today, I feel very grateful for all the love I am receiving. It has put me in a positive mind set. The outpouring of support and kindness fuels me to keep pushing and conquer this disease, no matter how tough things may become.

As my spirit has continued to soften, I've let my guard down. I've begun saying, "I love you" more often. I say it to family, friends, and even strangers sometimes. It's not simply lip service—I really feel it in my heart. I'm now able to see beyond a person's external being and hone in on what lies inside their heart. As time has marched on, I've noticed more people responding with kindness. Sometimes these sentiments come from the most unexpected sources; from people who are usually very guarded and stern. A few years ago, a colleague of mine gave me a gift for Christmas. Knowing how affectionate I was, when she handed me the gift she said, "and don't start hugging or kissing me, just accept it." She visited me a couple of years later, as I was undergoing treatment. Much to my surprise, she hugged me several times. What's more, she said, "I love you" during a phone conversation. This once again confirmed my belief in the boomerang affect. What we put out there, we attract toward ourselves. If an action is generated from the heart it will always be returned to you in some form.

Love can be offered at any time. We can offer it when we are cooking, cleaning, working, or driving. I think of times when I have intentionally poured love into the food I'm preparing for my family. The recipe remained the same, but somehow the food tasted better, and was eaten with more enthusiasm than normal. This seems prevalent in the food industry as well, where I have worked for years. The cooks who put love into their cooking always produce the best cuisine. Similarly, this principle applies within our homes. Where love resides, so does joy, peace, and unity.

I have driven aggressively in traffic many times, only to arrive late at my destination, feeling miserable. As I became aware of this I decided to experiment by sending out the vibe of love to the drivers around me. Doing so often yielded good results; fellow drivers would either let me into traffic, allow me to pass, or offer some gesture of kindness (rather than the one-finger salute I used to receive!). I cannot overstate that when we pour love into the things we do, it is usually returned to us.

Although love is powerful, it is not perfect. Many times in life we have to walk away from people we love, not because our love has ceased; rather, their presence in our life is no longer healthy. When there is irretrievable dysfunction and imbalance in any relationship, it is time to acknowledge it and gently walk away. I have experienced this a few times myself with people very close to me. The truth is, over time, some people change, and relationships follow suit. This is perfectly okay. We are constantly evolving as human beings, and our needs, desires, and priorities are in flux. One cannot force love upon someone or forcibly request it. When you are selling your soul, dignity, and self-respect in the name of love, then you know you have ventured too far. The bottom line is this: if it hurts to love someone and is stunting your growth, it is not worth your sanity. Give yourself and the other person the freedom to move on. Sometimes a little bit of time and space heals. If it doesn't, remember that by letting go you are creating space for someone more suitable to enter your life. The universe never abandons us.

When we allow ourselves to just be, we open pathways within us that lead to our gifts. I have been blessed with the ability to connect with others very easily. I encounter people in all kinds of places and circumstances who will share the most intimate details of their lives with me. It may be family problems, trauma they suffered in childhood, or their inability to heal pain so they can move forward. I seem to attract all kinds of people—young, old, women, men, rich, or poor. It doesn't matter who they are, I always put myself in their position and utilize my compassion compass. I see this as an internal guide I possess, which not only leads me to those in need of emotional comfort, but also shows me how to help them heal. In the moments that we connect, the person feels they're being listened to, understood, and that they're not crazy. Validating their feelings is important, and it's also an opportunity to show them a way out. We don't always have a safe place to divulge our pain. My belief is that when we offer comfort and love to those around us, we are giving them hope and the impetus to let go and reimagine themselves.

Imagine how beautiful our world could be if we offered our hearts and hands to others in a non-judgmental manner. Think of how people would blossom—think of the joy we could generate! Love is boundless and does not discriminate. It knows no colour, race, religion, gender, or social standing. Love brings happiness, strengthens souls, and motivates those to aspire; it eases burdens, heals ailments, and gives hope. Learning to give and receive love openly is not always easy, but it is the gateway to peace and ultimate happiness.

BEFRIENDING FEAR
BY ORIT GAL

Fear used to consume me. With each fever, alarm bells would ring; with each headache, thoughts of another tumor invaded my mind. I have come a long way since then, so why rehash my experience instead of putting it all behind me? I share my story because doing so allows me to keep healing and letting go. If I didn't have the courage to talk about it, I wouldn't have been able to see the light at the end of the tunnel, the light that helped me survive cancer.

In October of 2014, I received a call from my family in Israel telling me that my mother had taken a bad fall and would need surgery. She was eighty-two years old at the time, and in generally good health. After hearing the news, the first thing I did was book a flight from Toronto to Israel to be by her side. Just prior to leaving, I had a routine mammogram scheduled that I was all too happy to cancel. When the hospital asked me for an alternate date, I quickly brushed it off, saying that I'd reschedule upon my return.

When I arrived in Israel, I was met with the reality that my mother would never be the same. She had not only broken her pelvis, but had also suffered a minor stroke from hitting her head. Because of her age and medical condition, the doctors were afraid to give her the anesthesia she would need to undergo surgery. Instead, my mother was left to cope with immense pain. In one fell swoop, she was transformed from an independent, vibrant woman to an inactive, dependent one. The ferocious woman I'd known—the one who'd grown up in a chaotic household with fourteen brothers—was nowhere to be found. As I sat by her bedside watching her sleep under sedation, I couldn't help but reflect on the hardships she had endured. Nostalgia took over, and memories of my mother and my childhood came rushing back.

My mother's parents had immigrated from Syria to Israel when she was a young girl. They worked hard to make a life for their many children, and her own parenting style was heavily influenced by her upbringing. My mother learned from her parents that harsh punishments would follow those children who didn't obey. Needless to say, Mom didn't have it easy—until she met my father.

My father was a handsome, German-born Jew. During World War II his parents miraculously managed to save him from the Nazi concentration camps by smuggling him and his brother into Israel. Unfortunately, his parents didn't make it out of Germany alive and were slaughtered in the Holocaust. My father quickly went to work as a councillor for young boys on a Kibbutz (a collective community based in agriculture). He had come from an upper class family in which music and culture were very important. He played the violin and harmonica, and spoke many different languages. He was an Ashkenazi Jew, meaning a Jew of Eastern European descent. Overall my father was a very educated man, especially in comparison to my mother.

Coincidentally, my mother's brother also lived on the same Kibbutz as my father. And not only that, but my father happened to be my uncle's councillor. One day, my mother was ordered to deliver some clothes to her brother, and that's when their paths crossed. My father was instantly love-struck by my mother's exotic Arabian appearance. She was a natural beauty, with long, silky black hair and dark eyes. He didn't care who she was or what side of the tracks she came from. All he saw was her, and that's all he ever needed.

The little remaining family my father had left criticized their relationship, saying an Ashkenazi should never marry a Sephardic Jew. "The girl lacks culture and education. She can barely read, not to mention write!" But love won, and he married her anyway. He had already made up his mind that she was to be his wife and the mother of his children. Despite her lack of education, she was wise, with street smarts owed to her arduous upbringing. My father tried to help her adapt to his more sophisticated way of life but he didn't always succeed. My mother's deep-rooted, rough demeanor was stronger than my father's will to change her. Now that I'm older, I understand my mother, and have come to love and accept her strength of character. But I didn't always have the same admiration for her.

My mother's militant approach to managing her household instilled the fear of God into me as a child. Sometimes I found myself sitting quietly in the hallway of our house, hoping and praying she wouldn't need anything more from me. One day I came home scratching my head, knowing I had caught lice from the kid who sat beside me in class. I tried everything to remediate the problem myself out of fear of what would happen should she find out. But eventually I had no other option; I had to ask her for help. As my mother examined me in the tub, I sat there shivering in fear. In anger she proceeded to cut off all my hair with madness in her eyes. She kept cutting as short as possible until she reached my scalp. But she didn't stop there. She took oil and vinegar and smeared it all over my head. I was only a little girl, and instead of showing some compassion and tolerance, she had become a madwoman. Next she wrapped my head in newspaper and transferred me to a chair in the middle of our living room. There, she made me wait for a few hours, my head burning in pain from the vinegar. As I sat there inhaling the strong odour I thought I was going to die.

A few hours of sitting there in pain gave me courage to retaliate.

"It's just lice!" I finally barked.

"Just lice?!" she rebutted. "Shame on those who have lice. In my house, there will be no such thing!"

The next morning, I got to stay home from school, which I was very happy about since I would surely be made fun of by all the children. In my defense, my lioness of a mother stormed right into my classroom and demanded from the teacher and principal that every child be checked for lice. Her daughter was not to return to school until all students were checked and declared free of lice. Everyone was afraid of her. But they all did exactly as they were told.

When I finally returned to school, my friends asked me pitifully, "Why did she cut your long, beautiful hair so short? Why didn't she take you to a proper barber?" I didn't have a response, so I just kept quiet.

Memories of my mother continue to overwhelm me now. I know she loved me and wanted nothing but the best for me, yet everything I did was harshly critiqued. Every afternoon when I came home from school—before even saying hello to me—she would check to see what homework I had that day. I'd immediately have to sit down to work on it. Once completed, if something didn't look right, she would tear up my work and make me start over. She did this without hesitation. My mother made me so angry, yet I didn't dare say anything. Instead, I lived in fear, keeping my emotions bottled up.

On the days we did laundry I would sit for hours, washing, ironing, and folding to make sure everything was perfect and wrinkle-free. Since I slept in the living room, every night I would wait for my family to go to bed before preparing the couch by putting a clean sheet on it. One night, since we had just finished folding the clean laundry, I decided not to put a sheet down and left it folded so as not to wrinkle my hard work. My mother unexpectedly came to say goodnight and noticed that I had not made my bed properly. She immediately started screaming at me. "That's how you mock all my hard work? Get out of the house!" I ran out, afraid the beating would begin. My brothers heard the screaming and came outside to sit with me along the fence lining our property. They sat with me half the night until she finally decided to let us back in. My dear father tried to convince my mother to stop screaming and relax. He was by nature more quiet and calm. He never cursed, slapped, or yelled—the complete opposite of her. But his hands were tied. He was no match for her in the discipline category, and his efforts were futile.

Amongst the heartache and pain, there were also good little moments I shared with my mother. Without her example, I wouldn't be who I am today—an independent, hard-working and selfless person who gives without expecting something in return. I've never been dependent on others.

I sat watching my strong, independent mother having to rely on doctors and nurses now, and it broke my heart. I spent two weeks in the hospital caring for her day and night, but after two weeks I had to go home and get back to my life. My mother was transferred to a rehab facility and my sister and brother took shifts looking after her. This is the price I paid by moving to Canada. I wasn't able to be there for her the way I wanted.

As I was saying goodbye, my mother took my hand and didn't let go. She held it with a firm grip and said, "I love you; please don't leave me. I don't want to be alone." There I was, her youngest daughter, not so young anymore, being held on to by her mother who refused to let go. I looked at her and said, "I love you too, Mom. Everything will be fine. I will be back soon. You're not alone! My brother and sister are here and they will take good care of you."

Upon arriving home I went back to my daily routine and completely forgot about looking after myself. I had forgotten about my mammogram until I got a call from the hospital secretary asking me if I wanted to reschedule the test. I paused on the phone for a moment, contemplating whether or not I even had time to go. The nice secretary interrupted my thoughts. "This is important. Just get it over with." I was surprised by her level of caring compared to my indifference.

"Okay," I said. "I will go."

It was on a Monday that she called, and the test took place that Friday at 9:00 PM. My husband came with me for the test. After the test was done, the nurse came out and said I needed another x-ray, and then another, and then another. Each time I didn't think anything of it. By Monday morning on my way to work, I got a phone call from the hospital. "You urgently have to come back today. We saw something in the scan and we'd like to take a biopsy."

I returned to the hospital without informing anyone that I was going. I did the test and they told me that I'd have to wait a few days for the results. While driving with a friend, the phone rang. I missed the call and the message was from the surgeon's office. They informed me that I must call the clinic without delay, today if possible. When I reached the hospital I tried to tell the nurse how busy I was. She immediately said, "No! This is urgent and you must see the doctor today because he's going on vacation." I didn't tell my husband and just planned to take care of it myself. Luckily for me, the girlfriend I was with wouldn't let me go alone. Even with the urgency from the hospital, I still didn't believe anything was wrong. I was typically the one supporting, assisting and taking care of others. I couldn't imagine being on the receiving end of the spectrum.

When we arrived at the clinic I checked in at the front desk. The secretary was so nice and treated my friend and me like two lost children who had wandered in off the street. We were seen by the doctor very quickly. His office was beautiful and luxurious. Just as I was admiring my surroundings, the doctor looked at my friend and me before asking, "How do you feel?" I told him everything was fine. Then he started talking.

"Your test results indicate a tumour in your left breast, but it's not large and we believe we caught it in time," he said.

"So what now, Doctor?" I asked. "What does this mean?"

"You will need surgery to remove the tumour, and then you'll undergo radiation. The cancer appears to be small and does not seem to have spread anywhere else."

My initial response was "No problem." Then I started to laugh. "Are you sure this isn't a mistake?" I asked. "No, this is not a mistake." I informed him that I hadn't spoken with my husband yet, and that he would want to ask his own questions. "Not to worry; I will answer all of his questions and will make myself available to talk."

We left the doctor's office gobsmacked, not knowing what to say to each other. My friend finally turned to me and said, "Everything will be fine." I agreed.

That night, as my husband stood there speaking to me casually about his day, all I could think about was how to tell him the news I'd been given, and that we had an appointment with the doctor tomorrow.

"So...listen. I had an appointment with a surgeon today and I need to have surgery. They found a small lump in my chest and...of course it's nothing..." I laughed nervously.

"It's always the same with you. You laugh at everything. This really isn't funny," he responded with a look of judgment in his eye. "It's not nice to joke about these things."

"This time I'm not joking," I answered.

"What lump?" he asked, with fear in his voice.

"We will have all our questions answered from the doctor tomorrow," I reassured him. "Everything will be fine."

The next day, we went to the doctor and listened, talked, asked, and decided. The doctor then booked my surgery for the following Tuesday. Until then, I was put through a series of painful tests, one in which they injected radioactive dye into me without anesthesia. I asked myself how anyone could live with such pain. Apparently you can. I decided not to let the pain defeat me. I chose mind over matter, all the way.

My sister came from Israel to be by my side at the hospital. My husband, my best friend, my sister--everyone cried but me. Somehow, I was the only one who kept my composure. After five hours of surgery, we were given the news. I had a small, but aggressive tumour growing in my left breast that had spread to the surrounding lymph nodes in my armpit. The plan of attack was a series of chemotherapy, followed by radiation and some additional surgery. This was my only option if I was to be successful in beating this disease.

Shocked and scared, I said "Yes, let's do it." I still had too much living to do; I was definitively choosing life.

I met with the oncologist for testing, preparation and further discussions that helped clarify exactly what would be happening. She explained that, "Your hair is going to fall out after the first round of chemo, then your eyebrows, eyelashes, and then your fingernails and toenails. You will also experience pain in your bones." I could hardly believe that I was going to deteriorate from a healthy woman, one who was used to supporting everyone around her, to a dependent, "ill" one.

At first, I decided not to share my cancer diagnosis with anyone. I went to see my hairdresser Michael, who had been begging me to cut my hair short for years. I had always refused, scared to even part with a centimetre of hair. This time, I asked him to chop it off and donate it.

"Are you okay?" he asked in shock.

"Yes, cut it short and donate it to a good cause."

"A girl with such lush, black hair, who has always been afraid of scissors? Something must be wrong."

He obviously wasn't going to just accept my answer at face value, instead insisting on knowing what was behind my out-of-character request.

I had to tell him. "I have breast cancer, but it's not that bad. I figure it's just easier to lose short hair than long hair," I said, matter-of-factly.

Michael stood for a few moments in silence, not knowing what to say or how to say it. Finally, he said, "Wow, life can be so unpredictable. What happened? Why?"

I tried to reassure him not to worry, that everything was going to be all right. In general I found it difficult to tell people I had been diagnosed with cancer. Most didn't know what to do with the news, how to react. Some looked at me in bewilderment, wondering, "How much time do you have left?" Then there were those who felt compelled to tell me of all the people they knew with cancer who had survived. Through it all, I certainly came to know who my true friends were. Some disappeared, while others offered to help but didn't really mean it. Then there were those who really surprised me for the better.

I endured chemo treatments every three weeks. On treatment days, I would get up, get dressed, put on makeup, and tell myself, "Choose to live and move on."

My best girlfriends were incredibly supportive. They kept me company during my treatments, singing and chatting about nothing. They kept the conversation light and positive as if it was just normal girl talk. My wonderful sister came from Israel and sat beside me for my last three treatments. She pushed me to look forward, to the future—instead of backward, to the hardship.

After each treatment, I had three hard days in which I could not get out of bed. Vomiting ensued, followed by terrible pain in my bones. At the end of those three days, though, I went back to work as if nothing had happened. I didn't tell anyone anything! I bought a wig that looked like my natural hair, and went about my business feigning normalcy. I hid my illness well because I didn't want to be met with a wave of pity.

The most emotional event for me was when my hair fell out. I was at home, alone. Suddenly I touched my head and the hair remained in my hands. I stood in front of the mirror and tears ran down my cheeks. I took a black garbage bag and picked up all the hair. At that moment I desperately longed for my mother. "Mommy, where are you?" Oh, how I longed for just one more embrace, one more affectionate touch.

At this point on my path to survival, my mother was confined to a wheelchair and knew nothing of my illness. Her mind still worked but her body had been deteriorating since her fall. On our daily phone calls, I'd encourage her and listen to her disappointment in me for not being there for her. I just kept telling her I'd be there soon.

Once I completed chemotherapy I began radiation. I didn't think anything could be worse than chemo. I went through radiation every day for thirty-five days from my breast up to my armpit, using a special machine that prevented it from affecting my heart. Each session took ten minutes and in those moments it felt like a million thoughts ran through my mind. At first, the sessions were pretty painless, but then, after several treatments, my nightmare began. My skin turned black—burnt to a crisp—and I suffered terrible, scorching pain.

After one particularly painful session, my sister and I stopped at a supermarket on the way home. There, on the shelf, was a lone stem from an aloe plant. My sister picked it up and began to cry. "God loves you," she said. "This will help you heal." She asked the cashier if there were any more leaves like that. "No," she replied. "I have no idea how that got there."

Throughout that day my sister cut pieces from the aloe branch, put them in the fridge, and then rubbed my body with it. Amazingly, the aloe vera really worked to relieve the burning. I made it through thirty-five terrible radiation treatments, burnt, wounded, and tired. But the suffering didn't seem to end there. More tests, more treatments followed, and all I desperately longed for was to get back to my old way of life, and more importantly, to go see my mother.

While I managed my treatments, my mother was waiting for me in Israel, wondering why I hadn't come to visit again since her fall. As soon as I was physically able, I returned to my favourite place, my childhood home. There she was—the woman who used to be so strong, so powerful, now sat in a wheelchair in the courtyard of her nursing home. My mother was so weak that she wasn't even capable of moving her head. As soon as I saw her I ran to her and hugged her, tears pouring down my face.

"It's me, Orit," I said. No response.

After a few seconds she said, "I don't know you. Who are you?" At first I naively thought that she didn't recognize me because of my hair, but when I realized that wasn't the case, it felt like someone had just stabbed me in the heart. My own mother didn't recognize me anymore. My sister told me to wait until morning, that she will rest, reset, and remember.

We went back to my sister's house and I couldn't stop crying. All I could think of was the image of my mother sitting helpless in her wheelchair, practically unresponsive. She had been refusing to eat and had seemingly decided to give up on life. I couldn't help but think about myself, and about what I had just been through fighting my cancer—never willing to give up, just so I can stay here another day, another week, another year. My mother, on the other hand, had already sealed her fate.

The next day, I arrived early in the morning to visit her again and this time she was sitting in her wheelchair looking beautiful and clean. Here was my chance to try again. "Mom, do you know who I am?" I asked. All I desperately wanted was for her to recognize me and call me by my name. In that moment, she looked at me, took my hand, and began stroking it with tears in her eyes. "You're my little girl who came to visit me. What happened to your beautiful hair? Why did you cut it all off?" Overwhelmed with excitement, I couldn't even react; I just clung to her and took in as much of the moment as I could.

Two days later, while visiting a friend of mine in Israel, I got an urgent phone call telling me to come back to be by my mother's side. My heart knew why they were calling but my head refused to believe. When I arrived I saw the sadness on my siblings' faces, and I realized that my mom was waiting to say goodbye to me. She went to bed that night and never woke up. Everyone was by her side. She looked so beautiful, so peaceful, without a wrinkle on her face. She looked like an angel. I hadn't been there for so many important moments. I hugged her and asked her to forgive me for the distance I had put between us. I told her I loved her and that I always would.

Cancer has changed my life completely. Through my disease, I have begun to understand the meaning of the little things in life. I've learned to appreciate what I have and not take anyone or anything for granted. I've even developed a love for my adopted country, Canada. Here, I'm surrounded by good people, including the supportive hospital staff who gave me the strength to continue on my long road to recovery. I joined a support group where one woman in particular said something that stuck with me: "A healthy mother is a happy mother." This statement means more to me now than it ever could have in the past.

As mothers, we tend to become preoccupied with every little hitch in our children's lives, often overlooking our own health. We want to ensure our kids' happiness and success, even at the expense of our own. However, it's a two-way street; children also wish happiness and fulfillment for their mothers. With the help of that teaching moment, I learned to make myself a priority. I realized that the greatest gift I could give my husband and children was that of a healthy and happy wife and mother. But in order to uncover my best self, I had to find a way to manage the overwhelming fear that was controlling my emotional and physical health. Thinking long and intensely about my mother finally brought me to a realization: I must accept the unpredictability of life as part of its beauty. Instead of being ruled by fear, I have chosen to befriend it.

Though I feared my mother's harsh and unpredictable discipline as a child, our love for each other had no boundaries. Moreover, that fear didn't stop me from having a joyful childhood that I would relive all over again in a heartbeat. I see my mother as a perfect metaphor for my life. They are both imperfect, but that doesn't make me love them any less. They are both unpredictable, but fearing their unpredictability never stopped me from wanting to learn more from them. They are both harsh at times, but that just makes me appreciate the good moments even more. Fear is a small price to pay when you love someone as much as I loved my mom, and cherish life enough to conquer obstacles to happiness. Fear did not define my relationship with my mother—love did. That is proof that fear can coexist with my positive feelings, instead of dominating them. I applied the same logic to my cancer-related fear and realized how much energy I'd expended fighting and resisting. So, I stopped fighting and accepted it as part of me. Fear still accompanies me every day, but in order to enjoy life to the fullest, I must look on the bright side. I now view fear as a cautious companion who sometimes slows me down, but can never stop me. As I turn the pages in the book of my life, I have learned to stay hopeful that the next chapter will be a wonderful one.

COLOURING OUTSIDE THE LINES
BY JAIME LUND ONOFREY

"The only thing permanent in life is change."
—Heraclitus

I'll take you back to the day that changed everything for me. It was the day that brought me to the edge of my existence and back again. I was catapulted into a download from the universe that upgraded my inner software—not unlike the matrix in the sense that I was given the proverbial red pill. Once awakened to the truth, I would never be the same again.

Life was almost taken from me, and in coming face to face with death, the quintessential secrets of life were revealed to me in a profound multilayered process I've come to call spiritual alchemy. It was through almost dying that I really began to live.

I had just celebrated my twentieth birthday and had arrived late the night before to the rustic bungalows that lined the azure blue of the Gulf of Thailand. What was supposed to be a romantic getaway quickly turned into my worst nightmare.

That morning I awoke to the most pristine expanse of perfection and palm trees, put my feet up to take it all in, and ordered a breakfast dish almost entirely of seafood and a side of beer. My vacation had officially begun. Only a couple hours later I began to feel horribly ill. As it turned out the fish was bad. It was assumed to be food poisoning.

My vision began to blur as I crawled on all fours to the water's edge. I needed to feel the water on my burning skin and hoped that it would wash away the unbearable pain in my abdomen. As the water lapped up onto the shore it crossed my mind that it may be the last time I would feel the ocean. The mere thought that I might never see the ocean again brought me rapidly into the present moment. I savored its imperfect perfection. *No, no, how silly*, I thought to myself. *Don't be so dramatic, it's just food poisoning. This too shall pass.*

I was weary from days of travelling, and had escaped Bangkok, Thailand's capital, via an ensemble of transportation. The bumpy and excruciatingly long bus ride to the southern majesty of Southeast Asia had made me a master at holding my fluids. Lonely Planet Travel Guide neglected to inform me busses do not stop for people who have to pee. So I drank virtually no water, in the hopes that my amateur bladder would last the journey. I quickly became dehydrated and puffy.

Getting onto the ferry to cross the ocean to Ko Samui Island, I curled up and had a catnap on my backpack. We were a mix of mostly young foreigners so I felt at ease as I drifted into the type of sleep that you could stay in forever. My body began to exhale.

Months of hard work in the Japanese prefecture of Fukushima had left me weary. I'd learned to write and speak Japanese well enough to teach and live day to day, but months of a second language in a foreign country had taken its toll. I was working in the Bandai 7, representing Canada teaching skiing during the '98 Winter Olympics. I was strong, and in vibrant health…or so I thought.

I had been in to see the doctor several times, sent away with prescriptions in neatly folded packages, but the doctors didn't really seem to be clear on what I was suffering from. I recall one doctor in particular mumbling *"Gaijin Gaijin"* (foreigner) and then sending me on my way. Ultimately I decided I was homesick, as no clear illness appeared to ail me. I planned for a vacation in the soothing sun before heading home to see my family.

If we could live our lives backwards, all the signs were there. My swollen hands were speaking to me; my dull, lifeless eyes looking back at me in the mirror persuading me to take notice of the nagging feeling in my gut and protruding round inflamed belly. The fogginess in my brain was clouding the obvious. Something was seriously wrong and a vacation to the middle of nowhere was not the answer. The perfect storm was brewing.

When night fell and I was no longer finding solace at sea, I resorted to propping myself up with the toilet bowl. The shower, conveniently located above, was running over my body. Tim, my boyfriend and travel companion, was as green a traveller as I was. He was somewhere between restrained panic and exhausted comatose. He kept waking up as though a foghorn had gone off each time I let out a shriek of pain.

I knew something was terribly wrong when I started to lose my vision. When Tim saw blood in the toilet, the bell on his panic button started to ring him into full-blown red alert.

My consciousness was in and out of places it had never been before. The clock struck midnight as Tim tried to find help in the middle of the night. When he returned dangling keys in front of me I had a feeling the adventure was just beginning. I was in too much pain to care. In classic Tim style, he was still calm under pressure with a small grin on his face.

I was immediately scooped up and put on the back of the scooter. Tim held me with one arm while he dodged deep potholes and falling coconuts. He had "borrowed" the scooter from the beach huts where we were staying when he was unable to find any help. Mission accomplished after finding a wall of numbered keys and conveniently matching scooters.

Miraculously, Tim managed to get us to the hospital in one piece. As I was being carried into the bright emergency room, it felt as though a knife was stabbing me over and over again in my abdomen. Tim attempted to explain what was happening to the attendant, who only spoke Thai. The pain was so intense and excruciating I would rather have died in that moment than endure it.

My body had the animation of a Raggedy Anne Doll. Several nurses ushered around us, wearing uniforms that looked like they had just stepped out of the '50s. They kept looking at one another with nervous glances as they took blood. They didn't think I was going to make it. These are very specific looks I've come to know quite well.

It was the first time in my life that I had the very real, very tangible feeling that death was lurking over my shoulder.

I closed my eyes for a moment only to be startled by an elderly man, in what I would guess was his late seventies. He had a timeless quality and emanated an inexplicable kindness and wisdom. Standing at about 5'2, he had to stand on his tip toes to examine me. He wore a strangely short tie and was missing several teeth. He smelled like earthy herbs and a distinct spicy aroma that could have been his cologne but was more likely his last meal.

I could barely make out the details of his sweet wrinkly face. But I could see his eyes behind thick smudged glasses. He was a retired surgeon, as I would learn, and had studied medicine in Britain. He knew some English and knew how to perform surgery, so they rang him up. He was the best chance I had.

I recall it like it was yesterday, those first words I heard as he held my hand, and patted it gently with his other hand.

"You, surgery, now...or you die. Okay?"

He said it almost as if I had a choice, which I realized quickly, I didn't. I knew that if I had surgery there I would probably never wake up.

"Please...fly me to Bangkok," I begged, in a barely there, but very desperate voice. I figured if I could at least get to Thailand's capital I might at least have a chance of survival. He paused for a moment and squeezed my hand a little tighter. With deep compassion he peered over the top of his spectacles and said,

"You fly...you die."

So that was that. He smiled a smile that I will never forget to this day. His expression said, *there is no time for questions, let's do this.* He kept smiling and nodding his head simultaneously. I froze as the reality of the situation settled and I realized that it would take a miracle for me to come out of this alive.

I was wheeled down what felt like a never-ending hallway. I was crying but my face wasn't moving. It was as though my heart was being squeezed so tightly that tears were simply falling out of my eyes. They rolled down my cheeks in large elephant-sized globes. I was in shock and my mind began to reel with all of the possible outcomes of the inconvenient truth of my situation.

It felt like my heart was ready to burst through my chest. I wasn't ready to die. All the things I hadn't done or seen or said came flooding into my mind. What was death like? Would it hurt? How would my family cope with the news?

The doors to the operating room swung open with urgency. There was a team waiting, hurriedly preparing the space and speaking in Thai. As soon as the wheels stopped moving and I was slid onto the operating table, all I could feel was the cold steel underneath my body. Everything slowed down as though I was suddenly running through molasses in slow motion. And there it happened. I became completely and utterly paralyzed with the deepest fear I've ever known. I had not made friends with death. I was not at peace with letting go. I was not ready to die.

I was going to die alone, in Thailand, with no one to say goodbye or hold my hand. I was in a room full of strangers who didn't speak my language. I was in abject terror down to the bone. The urge to get up and run and scream and escape was so overpowering but heavy Velcro straps at my shoulders, hips, and legs strapped me down.

Undoubtedly, medical practice in a country like Thailand is quite different from how things would be done back home. I could hear the Velcro being peeled back on the surgical set. It sounded like thunder. Everything became amplified and slowed down as though I was under water. The texture of the air changed. The room became grey. Steel knives glimmered with the reflection of the bright lights overhead. A mint green, starchy sheet with a giant hole in it cracked above me. As it slowly wafted down towards my body, the light from the surgical lamp above filtered down through the hole.

There was an overwhelming infusion of smells. Iodine was swabbed onto my belly. It looked like blood and smelled even worse. What looked like a giant sharpie pen was uncapped and used to draw the incision line on my skin, which started above my belly button and went all the way down to my pubic bone, then crossed horizontally. Surgical tic-tac-toe. The sound of rubber gloves snapped inside my ears, voices lowered as the nurses talked amongst themselves. Clicking sounds, squirting sounds, more smells. Then I heard the nurse tap on a needle with her finger.

The bright lights blinded me as they were steered directly over me. All the sounds and voices and movement faded away into the darkness outside the light. I stared into that light until what I can only describe as falling into it. And then, suddenly, there I was, outside of my body looking down on myself. I could see the entire room, all of the people in it, all of the details and corners. I was watching the surgical team operate on me from above. I could see that I was dying. They were fighting hard to save my life, but they were losing.

My feelings of stress and anxiety were gone and the paralyzing fear of death evaporated. The pain and struggle were gone too. There was an immense peace and an incredible sensation of expansion, as though I could fill every corner of the universe. I didn't experience myself as separate with anyone or anything. The space was magnetized, magnified. There was a clear sense of oneness. My wisdom was in its fullest.

My experience was one of absolute love, like nothing I had ever felt before. There was nothing to be feared there. The experience showed me the formless nature of my being. The impermanence of my body, and the impermanence of everything we encounter in life.

Matter was merely a suggestion, as the dense reality of the physical world became porous. I moved through the space by my intension. I realized dying wasn't the hard part. The hard part was really living with the precious time I had been given.

It became crystal clear that the best way to travel through the journey of life is to un-clutch, to let go into the flowing river of life. To not sweat the small stuff, and to find simple ways to elevate my spirit and enjoy the moment despite what pain life presented.

Ultimately I was given a choice. I could let go of the body and life that I knew, or I could make the choice to live, to go back into my body, with the clarity of who and what I am. I had to begin the fight for my life, which I realized was more a battle of spirit and will. Supported by the forces that animated me, the miraculous became inevitable.

It would have been easier to release into that blissful world beyond the body. Instead, I chose to return, to what became a white-knuckled journey to reclaim my life. I was not a human being having a spiritual experience; I was a spiritual being having a human experience. I had secured my place in the cosmos. Now the task would be to integrate and connect my experience into the tangible. As it would turn out, being human was the hardest part.

When I woke up days later from surgery, the pain I felt was excruciating. After my interlude with infinity, being inside a body filled with trauma felt highly claustrophobic. It would have been easy to assume I had made a mistake to return. The contrast between such extraordinary expansion and formlessness, back to being in my physical body invoked intense nausea and vertigo. I came up against fear like a fire-breathing dragon that was just learning to walk.

It was a form of *spiritual whiplash*. I went from vapor to ice in 1.3 seconds, without the middleman of condensation. I still have memories of feeling like a plane crashing on the tarmac of my body as my soul landed.

Being wheeled into surgery days before, I was certain that this was not something I was going to wake up from. I'd heard horror stories before leaving home about travellers being kidnapped and their organs stolen. I looked around for a bed of ice and the note that says, "Call 911, we've taken your kidney."

It was impossible to move as I was strapped to a gurney, but my head rolled around taking in my surroundings. There was a jar on the bedside table filled with extremely questionable contents. Later, I would find out those contents were the gangrenous, toxic remains of my ruptured appendix.

The hanging bag above my head was all that sustained me, dripping a concoction of intravenous fluids and a cocktail of pain medication and antibiotics. I was not to eat or drink for weeks. My body had been filleted open and barely put back together. Several of my abdominal organs and about twenty-two feet of intestines were taken out of my body, hosed down and put back in again. I had gone septic and had peritonitis, which basically means I was filled with noxious poison that needed to be dutifully removed or the toxins would circulate to my heart and cause cardiac arrest.

My organs hung like barely attached chandeliers from draped internal ceilings. Eight staples in an incision that spanned vertically, right up my midline, allowed me to look right inside myself. I had been turned inside out: literally and figuratively. It was an absolute miracle I was alive.

Over the next month, I convalesced in the hospital room I would come to know intimately well. I came to know the cracks in the ceiling like an astronomer knows the constellations in the night sky. The window to the outside revealed an extraordinary scene of color, abundance and beauty. There was a palpable shift in my ability to be present and savor simplicity. The veil that once separated me from my surroundings had been pierced, and now I felt as though I was looking through the eyes of a newborn child. The world was filled with wonder and I was in awe of it. This awe was juxtaposed next to extraordinary pain and discomfort, but paradoxically, the pain seemed to enhance my experience of the now. It taught me to feel through the pain, to the beauty that sleeps inside of it.

While I wrote on my philosopher's stone, Tim continued to explore the island. I lay in bed and processed my new discoveries. He would come back from his island jaunts with pictures of wild adventures and share tales of the world outside. I was living vicariously through him as he described in detail the sights and sounds in this new world.

While he was experiencing the outer world, I was experiencing my inner one. Ironically life had taken me on the most unexpected adventures of my own, all without leaving the hospital bed. I began to experiment with the magnificent capacity of creativity and the brain and body's inability to know the difference between what we actually experience and what is imagined. The feelings that I attached to whatever I imagined brought the inner movies to life. I was directing the movies of my mind and changing my outer experience as I altered my inner reality.

I began to awaken to the power of my thoughts, and through the clarity of my intention, I began to bring my thoughts to life. It was an awesome experiment, and I was able to see how powerfully I can manifest and create when I am in a clear and present state. I began to visualize my healthy body walking around the room.

When I wasn't experimenting with my consciousness, I was reading the Book of Buddha. It was left beside my bed, much like a bible might be left in a hotel room bedside table. The book spoke about the cause of human suffering, which led me to study my own with great fervor. I was fascinated by my own suffering, and what tended to trigger it. Pain was inevitable, but suffering was a choice.

There were clear patterns emerging. That clarity gave me the courage to delve into what had caused me to suffer in the…gulp, *past.*

My struggles became my spiritual petri dish, as I tested the concepts against my own experience. Concepts on paper shifted into embodied visceral experiences as I became the proverbial guinea pig. I had become an accidental spiritual scientist. It was official—my near-death experience delivered me the red pill, and I could never go back.

The first test was to learn to laugh. If you have ever gone an extended period without laughing, you know how difficult it can be to learn to laugh again. It did not feel like riding a bike. My inner joy seemed to be in a sealed reservoir deep within me. It amazed me how pain had a way of taking over the lightness of being required to merely laugh. I was determined to access my inner child, the part of us that laughs effortlessly and often. I needed a way to get it to bubble up to the surface. I couldn't remember how. Thankfully, Tim, who had been instrumental in saving my life, was now charged with making me laugh about it.

The first time I was encouraged to go to the bathroom by myself it took me over twenty-five minutes just to get out of bed. Tim assisted me as I shuffled step by tiny step to the bathroom holding my IV stand as a cane. I couldn't eat, walk or go to the bathroom by myself. My tummy muscles had been incised and it was apparent. Walking without tummy muscles is much harder than one might think. They have a lot to do with holding us upright and helping to put one foot in front of the other. *One step at a time* became my mantra. It was more of a shuffle than a walk, but eventually, painstakingly, I made it and gingerly I was assisted to the *laughing pot*.

I was wearing what is now my infamous "cowboy and lasso" hospital gown. It was the couture du jour while recovering for all patients. I think it was Thailand's way of reminding us not to take things too seriously while our asses flashed from our gowns. I sat there for what seemed like an eternity hoping that my bits would begin to work again and I would hear that glorious tinkle sound.

Tim decided it was a good idea to put a snorkel and mask on me and take a picture holding an empty beer bottle while I sat on the toilet. The picture would later be titled ironically, "Best Vacation Ever." He began to laugh uncontrollably at the sight of me, sitting there on the throne in my cowboy jammies, snorkeling, "drinking a beer" (*I wish*...I would have chased after a mirage for a drop of water).

As he laughed, I started to laugh, my belly aching with the tightening of my muscles! Oh, the pain of laughter! It felt so good and hurt so much all at once! I begged him to stop making me laugh but it was contagious. The more he laughed, the more I laughed. The geyser had blown and the effervescent bubbling from deep within my soul released into uncontrollable chasms of blissful, painful, belly-aching, joy-filled laughter.

It certainly wasn't the best vacation ever, but I appreciated Tim's antics to lighten the mood. He was grateful I was alive, but as he saw it, my appendix had ruined our romantic getaway to these exotic islands.

He handed the Polaroid to me. As it dried and the picture fleshed forward, it felt very powerful to see myself appear from nothingness. There was an eerie quality to that moment; it was evident that the veil between life and death was thin. But ironically, the closer I was to death, the more alive I felt. The more I embraced the impermanence of this life, the more impact each moment carried. It didn't matter how big or small the moment—just that I was in it to the best of my ability, and that I was nowhere else but in my own life, in the present time, experiencing what was right in front of me.

Gratitude for my life, no matter what it looked like on the outside, became the currency that I have learned to trade moment to moment. If I was breathing and my heart was beating, then all I needed could be accessed through the Now. I had discovered the portal to my personal power. As it turns out, I didn't need to travel the world to find it; it was with me all along.

I felt in many ways like a little girl, returned to an innocence, magic and knowledge about the secrets of life. I felt like I had discovered the pearl inside life's proverbial oyster. Life had given me a great gift amidst what many saw as "bad luck."

I mentioned this to my doctor as he was cleaning my open drain holes for the infection with an oversized q-tip. It was fascinating to watch this massive cleaning stick disappear almost entirely inside my body. This was a ritual that was performed daily and we often looked for conversations to distract me from the procedure.

My Doctor smiled as he mopped up the mess around the wound with a cotton pad. He was clearly of the school of thought that believes *life is happening for us, not to us.*

He asked me if I had ever heard the story about the Buddhist monk and the farmer's son. I said no, and he went on to tell me an extraordinary story based on the idea that there is no such thing as good luck or bad luck, only our interpretation of what happens to us.

I came to know a sense of peace and comfort in his presence. When he left the room that same sense of love, peace and oneness that I had experienced out of my body while in surgery came flooding back in. I felt my heart soften and my body relax. It actually felt as though my heart was unraveling from a deep entrenched knot.

I took the first deep breath I had taken in years. I made the intimate connection between my breath and my life force. I breathed in that moment and it was all that existed. So much of my pain was in my perception. When I changed what I was focusing on, my whole world shifted. My breath became a doorway into my heart. When I would breathe into the expansion of my heart, my entire world would shift and soften. Space would return. This would create room for joy and peace and love. It showed me that what we resist persists, and that when we let go, we find true freedom in the present moment.

The path to healing had been an incredible journey. I had experienced a "coming home" like no other. Now, it was time to go home to my country, to my family and friends.

When I left the hospital a month later we took pictures with all the nurses and my miniature miracle doctor who had saved my life. An immense gratitude filled my heart for the people who had nursed me back to health. I had become a bag of bones in a wheelchair.

Thailand, being a Buddhist country, believes that organs are a sacred part of us. So, I was encouraged to take my appendix with me. It had adorned my bedside table for the last month, however, I lost it at customs on my way back to North America. I remember jokingly telling them, "It's a part of me!" Ironically I had become quite attached to it. It had become the totem, the honing beacon that brought me back home to myself. That tiny little viscera had become a great teacher. It had caused me so much suffering, and in the process I was delivered to myself.

Suffering is a choice. Life will hurdle innumerable opportunities to suffer. But if you're aware that suffering is what it is—catalytic by its very existence—then you have discovered the greatest key to the process of alchemy. Our entire existence is designed for us to be awakened.

When we can no longer change a situation, we are challenged to change ourselves. We cannot avoid pain, but we can choose how to cope with it, find meaning in it, and move forward with renewed purpose, like I did in Thailand. Make the most of your life. Do what makes you feel alive, and do what you love, because the truth is, we never know when our last day will be. We are not promised tomorrow. Anyone can die. Choose to be someone who has the courage to really live.

LOVE IS NOT SO BLIND
BY: MARIA REDA GOLDSTEIN

As the church doors opened, I stood there looking like a princess in my white custom-made wedding gown. Five hundred pairs of eyes rose to attention and watched in amazement as I proceeded to walk down the aisle, bouquet in hand. Instead of looking towards my groom, all I could see was the bright red exit sign overhead, but I ignored that sign just like I had ignored all the other ones.

This was supposed to have been the happiest day of my life, yet I felt nothing. Completely numb. Leading up to the ceremony the day was filled with hair, makeup, pictures, and excitement buzzing all around me. "Maria, you know, Mom and I want nothing more than your happiness," my father said as he tried to steal a meaningful moment with me during picture taking. He was trying to get my attention but I couldn't look him in the eye. I knew if he took a good look at me, he'd see that I knew I was making a mistake. He knew me too well. I couldn't let him see into my soul and I didn't have enough courage to admit that he was right about my feelings for Tony.

The party itself was fabulous—a big Italian wedding at Le Buffet Rizz, one of Montreal's finest banquet halls, served excellent food as we danced the night away to the music of a full blown orchestra. But after all the hoopla was over, and we said goodbye to the last of our guests, all that was left was the bride and groom. We were but two young children of twenty-four and twenty-one years old. Yes, I married a younger man. What's worse is that I knew I was in trouble as soon as the wedding and honeymoon were over. *How did I let it go so far?*

When I first met Tony, I was attracted to his rebellious nature. This young man was rough, brash, a high school dropout—just like those characters in the movies played by the likes of James Dean. Yet, I was attracted to this guy. He was different and I found him to be a challenge. Somehow I thought I would be the one who could show him the way, the one who would straighten him out and change him for the better. I thought deep down that if he saw what a wonderful family I came from that collectively we could have a good influence on him. Well, boy was I wrong. I really had no experience with men, and so my first mistake was thinking I could change someone.

My parents immigrated from Italy to New York in the late 1950s. I was born in the Bronx only nine months after their honeymoon. Shortly thereafter, they ended up settling in Montreal where my three younger brothers were born. My parents' unwavering love for each other was the type only seen on the big screen. Their relationship was one of pure devotion, and commitment—a real example from which to follow. Unfortunately, I didn't follow it. Introducing Tony to my parents for the first time should have been my first clue that he probably wasn't the best choice for me. My mom was sweet and unassuming, while my dad, who can be a little intimidating, looked at me funny which gave me the distinct feeling that he was not happy I was dating this guy. At first, they weren't too concerned, but when they realized I was serious about him they became very upset. We kept dating much to their chagrin. Given how young I was, my parents were hoping that this was just a phase and that I would wake up one day. That did not happen. In fact, their resistance to him made me more protective of the relationship. I wish I had had my parents foresight and wisdom.

For the next three years, my parents lived in distress. My dad did and said everything he could to discourage me from seeing Tony. He took me out to dinner, tried to buy me things, pleaded with me, did everything and anything to stop me from making the biggest mistake of my life. I thought, *How dare he tell me what to do*. "If the shoe were on the other foot, would you have stopped seeing Mom if someone forbade you?" I asked my father. He had no response. I wanted this guy in my life and nobody was going to prevent that from happening. Little did my parents know, but deep down I knew they were right. I saw things in him that scared me, but I was too hard-headed to admit it to myself. I simply decided to cast my doubts aside. If only I had listened to my heart instead of my stubborn head.

My parents were so upset about my relationship with Tony that I would catch them fighting about it. My mom had to persuade my dad to stop fighting with me about him because she was afraid they were going to drive me away. "Please, just let Maria do what she wants to do," my mom pleaded. My dad finally stopped resisting me. I wish now that he hadn't.

Tony and I got married on June 12, 1983. "What a beautiful couple," everyone said. Little did they know that I felt nothing and apparently, neither did he. Of course, we had some good times. We were young. Tony was a great dancer, and the life of the party. We were always out and about. He was a lot of fun, but let's just say, he was not husband material. Tony was hardly ever around. I remember feeling lonely even when he was in the same room with me. Our marriage was not really a marriage in the traditional sense of the word. Romance and affection were not on his radar and I never felt truly loved by him. We behaved more like two buddies hanging out. All the red flags that I had swept under the rug before we got married eventually came to the surface. I used to cry myself to sleep sometimes thinking, *Is this it? Is this what marriage is about?* I only wanted someone to love me, to be happy with, to share a life with. I used to dream of my knight in shining armour coming to rescue me from the hell that I was in.

Being as young and inexperienced as I was meant that I was also naive to Tony's extracurricular activities. He was always leaving to go out with "his friends" and coming home very late at night or in the early hours of the morning. All the while I was thinking, *Where could he be?* Questioning where he was would only lead to anger. He would punch the door, put a hole in it, hurt himself and blame it all on me.

In spite of Tony's anger and verbal abuse, in my mind, divorce wasn't an option. I had made my bed and I was going to lie in it. My parents had tried to dissuade me from seeing Tony, let alone marry him. I couldn't bear to hear, "I told you so," and I also held on to the hope that in time, things might get better. I saw potential in him. He had a rough side, yes, but I knew deep down that he had a heart. Being a part of a good, loving family like mine, I thought eventually he would grow to emulate my father and be more like him over time. I know now that leopards don't change their spots but I just wanted to tame him a little. *Was that too much to ask?*

Needless to say, eleven years of verbal and emotional abuse took its toll on me. I was not in a good place. My life felt surreal. The only thing keeping me sane was my job, my friends and my family. I kept my pain hidden very well. Everyone on the outside thought, "Oh my God, what a perfect couple." But the truth was that I was taking life day by day, hoping that time would make things better. It was one hell of a ride. As much as I love roller coasters, I wanted to get off this one badly, but didn't know how.

The final straw broke one night after Tony had been out all day. He came home, looked at me and said that he did not want to be married anymore. I looked at him in shock. I mean, if anybody was going to end this, it should have been me. As much as I know now that he was not marriage material, I blame myself just as much as him. I knew better. I was smarter than that. Smarter than him. How could I blame him for everything? I'm the one who chose to stay in an unhappy marriage for eleven years. To blame him and play the victim would be unfair. Every relationship is a two-way street. It was time for me to let go of the façade and admit reality.

As much as my parents tolerated the marriage, no one was surprised or upset when the news broke out that we were divorcing. In fact, I even saw the relief in my father's face. Likewise, I also felt like a weight had been lifted off my shoulders. I didn't have to pretend any longer. The charade was over and there were no more tears left to cry. I had done enough of that during the marriage. The only overwhelming feeling I had was fear. Fear of the unknown. *What was going to happen to me?* I didn't want to be alone. I was thirty-five years old when my marriage ended. Tony and I never had children together, which was a blessing, but I was really afraid of facing the rest of my life alone without someone to love.

"Thank God I have my daughter back," my father said when it was all over. "I'm just going to pretend like you've been locked up in prison for the last eleven years and just got released." It felt like my dad was trying to make light of a serious situation, which I didn't appreciate. There was nothing comical about what I was going through. "If I had to watch a movie based on your life with him, I don't think I would have been able to watch it without getting sick to my stomach." Wow, my poor dad somehow knew that I had been suffering in silence, yet I thought I had done a good job of hiding it. I never complained about Tony to my parents because I didn't want them to worry. I wanted to protect them from my pain. "I don't mean to insult you, Maria. You just deserve to be with a man who will love and take care of you." I knew my dad was right. At this point in my life it felt like the person my father was describing only existed in fairy-tales. *Where was my prince?*

While managing through my divorce I threw myself into my work as a means of distraction. As a customer service representative for the insurance company I worked for, I spoke with a lot of different brokers. Some were nicer than others, but there was one man in particular from Toronto named Jeff whom I spoke with regularly. Jeff had always stood out to me because of his beautiful deep voice and his sense of humor. I had never spent more than two minutes, if that, on the phone with him at any given time because I was all business. Although he often tried to strike up personal conversation with me, I always maintained my professionalism and never let my guard down, until one day when he caught me at my most vulnerable. I don't know if it was his demeanor or if I was totally out of my mind grieving over my divorce. Yet, on this particular day I must have unknowingly been transmitting my emotions through the phone. He mentioned that I sounded different. *Different?* I thought I was acting like myself. *What the hell did that mean?* Then he asked the magic question, "What's wrong?" That's all it took for the floodgates to open. There I was telling a total stranger about my broken marriage, divorce proceedings and how scary it all was. He mentioned that he had been through divorce himself and that believe it or not, it gets easier. I couldn't continue the conversation because I had to take other calls. He then suggested that if I needed to talk, I could call him at his home number. I have to admit that I really enjoyed the short conversation we had and it was really easy talking with him. I took his number down and put in my purse but then never actually thought to call him. A couple of weeks went by and my office phone rang. It was him.

"Why didn't you call?" he asked.

"I felt uncomfortable calling you," I said in response.

"Don't be silly. If you need someone to talk to, I'm happy to be that person for you."

It was towards the end of my shift so I didn't care how long I stayed on the phone with him. We spoke about dating, where I could meet men, my fear of being alone, my dream of having someone to love and to love me back. Then there was a long pause on the phone.

"Are you still there?" I asked.

"Yes," he said with a heaviness in his voice. "I wish I could pull you out of the receiver and give you a big hug." My heart sank. *What was going on here?*

After such an emotional phone call, I wanted so badly to speak with him again. I had to work myself up to call him as I was both nervous and excited all at the same time. It was around eight o'clock the following evening when I finally mustered up the courage to pick up the phone and dial his number. I thought he may be out, but he answered the phone in two rings. He sounded so happy to hear my voice which instantly put my mind at ease. We were on the phone all night. Conversation flowed from one topic to the next like a winding river. I had never seen time fly by so fast until that evening. We spoke about our lives, likes, dislikes, anything and everything. I couldn't believe it. We got along so well and it was so nice to have someone to talk to, someone who was actually listening to me. For the first time in a long time I had the attention I had been desiring. It amazed me how I was able to feel so open, so quickly. Then, to my amazement, I looked at the clock in front of me and it was 6:00 AM! What!? I told him the time and he was also shocked. I had to get off the phone because I had to get ready to go to work. How was I going to work without any sleep? I hung up, took a shower, got dressed and left. I got to work on time but I was so exhausted.

Jeff emailed me and called me twice that day to see how I was coping with no sleep. He was tired as well but missed me and couldn't wait to speak with me again. By the end of the day, I let him know that I really needed some sleep so we would have to talk later that night. I slept for a few hours and felt a lot better. We spoke again for a couple of hours but this time something was different.

"Could this be love?" I asked. My heart felt like it would leap out of my chest if I let it.

"Sure feels like it," he responded.

In just two phone calls we were actually falling in love. After that we couldn't get enough of each other. We spoke on the phone every day and every night. On my way home from work one night, I went through my bills and when I opened up the telephone bill, I thought I was going to die. The bill was $450.00. Oh my God! When I told Jeff about it he said he had a huge bill as well, but he was going to fix that. He bought a long distance package so that we could speak all day and all night. Step by step, this beautiful man was fixing everything wrong with my life and my heart.

Our little love affair over the phone went on for a few months. The puzzling thing about it all was that we had never actually met in person. This was the '90s after all. No Facebook or social media. I had no idea what he looked like. We described ourselves to each other but anyone could lie. Well, the mystery was solved when we decided to send each other photos. One day while we were on the phone, my doorbell rang and I excused myself to answer the door. It was a FEDEX guy with a special delivery. When I told Jeff what it was he said, "Great, those are my pictures." He asked me to open the envelope that very moment and tell him what I thought. I looked at the pictures and said, "Oh my God, yeah you're cute." However, I was really thinking, *Oh no, you're not my type!* Not only was his appearance not exactly the type I was typically attracted to, but he looked very conservative in a Wall Street type of way—serious and intelligent. How could I love this guy when I never dated someone so classy, professional, and mature? What would we have in common? He received my photos a couple of days later and was very flattering when he saw what I looked like. I was a little nervous about the whole thing at this point, but our looks and differences didn't matter. I was wholeheartedly in love with him. I realized then and there that this is how blind people must fall in love. I had fallen in love with Jeff's heart and soul, the things that truly matter.

The weekend we first met in person was magical. Jeff came to stay with me in Montreal and we both wished the weekend would never end. When he had to leave that Sunday evening, he stayed until midnight. He didn't want to leave me but he had to. He came to Montreal every other weekend for six months after that like clockwork. Our whirlwind romance progressed quickly from there, and it was around the six-month mark that I started to feel a little overwhelmed with it all. *Who falls in love over the phone?!* I thought to myself. Somehow it all felt too good to be true and I started to question everything. Jeff had been married twice before and had two little boys. In all honesty I was concerned I wouldn't be able to handle dating him long term. He had dated a lot more than me and was far more experienced than I was. His previous marriages didn't work out. What made me think this relationship had a chance? By comparison, I was insecure, scared and naive. Not to mention, he was Jewish and I was Italian. How was this possibly going to work? That's when I decided to call him up on a random Thursday afternoon and tell him I needed some space to think.

"You live in Montreal and I live in Toronto. How much space do you need?" he said in his typical sarcastic tone. Five hours later my doorbell rang. It was him. He had driven all the way from Toronto to Montreal straight from work on a whim just to prove a point. "Do you believe I love you now?" he said, as I stood there dumbfounded. That was Jeff: spontaneous and romantic. I couldn't deny or doubt my feelings any longer. He was the real deal.

The next step was meeting my family. He wanted to meet them sooner than I was ready for, but I was so proud to introduce him that I went along with his request willingly.

Jeff has always been very good at fitting in, and the weekend he met my family was no exception. I introduced him to my brothers and their wives first. There was no denying our love. It was written all over both of our faces. We all went out to dinner and had the best time together. By the end of the night my face hurt from smiling so much.

On the other hand, introducing Jeff to my parents for the first time was a little more nerve-wracking. On our way to my parents' home, I felt the need to warn him of my father's intimidating nature.

"Ah...so, I should warn you. My dad can be a little intimidating," I said timidly. "And no public displays of affection, please. They're old-school Italian."

"First of all, I can handle your father. And second, how can I not touch you all night?" he said with a chuckle.

"Just keep it to a minimum," I said smiling. We were like two teenagers who couldn't keep our hands off each other.

When we arrived, my mom welcomed us in her sweet, hospitable way. Then we went into the kitchen where my dad shook hands with Jeff for the first time. Before we could even make ourselves comfortable, my dad asked Jeff why he wanted to meet with them. I almost fell off my chair. He didn't waste any time getting to the heart of the matter. He wanted to know what Jeff's intentions with his daughter were. Well, Jeff and my dad spoke candidly about a number of things. At this point in our relationship, we had already decided that I was going to be moving to Toronto before the year end. My dad was not very keen about our plans. His only daughter moving five hours away with some guy she hardly knew—not his ideal situation. But what could he say? I was a thirty-six-year-old divorcée and as stubborn as I had always been. My mom was just happy that I had met someone nice and was happy to see me so happy. My dad was old-fashioned so he was not very happy about our plans for me to move to Toronto. However, he was relieved that I found a special man who took care of me. His only concern was my happiness and safety. I had that now. He really liked Jeff and ultimately believed he was a Godsend.

After only six months of dating long distance, I subleased my apartment, packed up my car, and said goodbye to my family and friends. I was moving to Toronto and was excited to start my new life. I said goodbye to my parents as if it was any other ordinary day. Some of my friends were skeptical and couldn't believe that I would just pick up and move to a new city with a man I hardly knew. I didn't care what they thought because I knew I was going to be with my soulmate. I was always a risk taker, but I felt really good about this relationship. Jeff was not a rebound; he was a new beginning. Being married to Tony for eleven years, I had missed out on true love and happiness. This was my chance. My knight in shining armour had come to save me after all.

Well, one week went by and after the novelty and excitement wore off, and reality set in as to what I had done, I started to cry. I missed my parents and friends terribly. I didn't have any family or friends in Toronto. Jeff held me close as I sobbed into his shoulder. "It's only a five-hour drive or a one-hour flight. You can go home any time you like," he said, consoling me. Jeff's family welcomed me with open arms. I had already met his children and most of his family by this point and they were all so nice to me. It took some time, but Toronto is now my new home.

Jeff and I established our routines as a couple. Winters were often spent vacationing in Florida with my parents. One particular trip, Jeff kept trying to get me to go for a walk on the beach to watch the sunset. Well, we were on the east coast of Florida where the sun sets behind the high-rise condos. My mother was in the middle of making dinner for us, and all I wanted to do was put my pajamas on and relax for the evening.

"Maria, let's go watch the sunset on the beach," Jeff said out of nowhere.

"But I'm hungry and besides, the sun sets behind all the condos. There's nothing to see right now," I responded.

"We'll eat later. There's plenty to see. It's a nice evening. Let's just take a walk on the beach." Jeff insisted.

As we were walking along hand in hand, I was starting to lose patience with why we were there.

"Do you like jewellery?" Jeff asked. I looked at him like there was something wrong with his brain.

"What are you talking about? You know I do. What girl doesn't?" I responded.

Next thing I knew Jeff was down on one knee pulling out a ring from his pocket. "Will you marry me?" he asked.

"Is this for real?" I was in shock. "Yes, of course I'll marry you!"

Well that shut me up. I don't think I spoke a word the whole way back up to the condo. For the first time I was speechless. Jeff personally designed and had my princess-cut engagement ring custom-made. When we got back up to my parents condo they were sitting there on the couch watch the door, eagerly waiting to celebrate. Everyone knew the proposal was coming but me. Jeff and I had been living together for seven years before he surprised me by proposing on the beach that day. I was over the moon!

We were engaged for a year before deciding to tie the knot on September 21, 2003. My wedding to Jeff was the complete opposite of my first in so many ways. Instead of feeling numb, I felt everything—every heartbeat, every tear, every speech, every loving touch. It was the most meaningful day of my life. Instead of a five-hundred-person wedding, we invited our immediate family consisting of just sixteen people. It was a private Jewish ceremony held at the Oakdale Country Club in Toronto. I wanted to get married in my husband's Jewish tradition. Jeff also surprised me with a violinist and an oyster bar. He spared no expense making our wedding as special as possible.

Through the twenty-two years that Jeff and I have been together, we've certainly had our ups and downs—times when I was scared we weren't going to make it. But our love for each other always transcended the doubt. The thought of living without him is unimaginable. Jeff is good to me, he cares about my welfare, he has my back and I have his. The only thing that I worry about is what if I lose him? What would I do without him? I could never replace my husband with another man because there is no other man like him. I love him. This is the only part about true love that scares me to death. I sometimes think it would have been safer to live alone, without finding love, but then I think to myself, *It is better to have loved and lost than never to have loved at all.*

When I got married for the first time at twenty-four, I didn't appreciate the seriousness of what I was doing. I must have been insane to have married someone I didn't truly love thinking that I could change him. My love for Tony wasn't blind; I just chose not to see. Of course, hindsight is twenty-twenty and there were so many red flags I should have paid attention to. Yet, I don't dwell on the time I wasted being married to Tony. I've let it go. It wasn't a mistake, but a life lesson to be learned from. It took me eleven years to open my eyes. Falling head over heels in love with Jeff was easy because my experience with Tony taught me to value my self-worth and take control of my own happiness, which ultimately allowed me to find my prince.

> *"You know you're in love when you can't fall asleep because reality is finally better than your dreams."*
>
> —Dr. Seuss

BREATHING THROUGH THE CHANGES
BY NELL ROSE FOREMAN

Letting go is a struggle of control. Think of an infant clutching a rattle so tightly that they're almost incapable of relinquishing their grip. As adults, we like to believe that we are in control of our lives. However, there are times when we're not, and, like that infant, we hold on to things in our lives too tightly. Admittedly, there have been many times in my life when I've behaved like that infant, gripping firmly and refusing to let go.

What I've come to realize over the years is that control is really an illusion; the only thing we can control is how we react to the circumstances of our lives.

When I examine my life today, I realize that what has shaped my character the most, are the struggles I've encountered, not the things that have come easily. Being a mother is a wonderful experience but also humbling. I view parenthood as a short moment in time where I get to connect with and guide these incredible spirits. It is a blessing to be a part of their lives, and I can honestly say they have taught me more about life than the other way around.

As a mother of five, I have so desperately wanted to keep my children safe from sickness, injury, bullying, and a broken heart – in essence, from anything negative. In my naiveté I believed for a long time that I could keep things in a neat little package that met my expectation of how things should be. But change was happening, whether I liked it or not and it was hard for me to let go.

I routinely experienced "normal" challenges with each of my children; I remember saying that if only they all had the same problem, I would be an expert! It wasn't easy to manage five kids' social calendars, doctor appointments, and schooling. But what really put me to the test as a mother were a series of extraordinary challenges.

One son had such severe Eczema that his skin would crack and bleed all over his body. When he was breastfeeding, I cut out several foods from my diet and switched to an organic cotton diaper service. I sought out the top doctors at Children's Hospital of Philadelphia (CHOP), both dermatologists and allergists. Nothing seemed to help. It was a constant battle of trial and error to make him as comfortable as I could. Finally, at age fourteen, he stopped bleeding and now maintains his Eczema with the help of his doctors.

Another of my sons had chronic ear infections as an infant that left him 80% deaf. As a result, he was diagnosed with Audio Processing Disorder and Dyslexia. We spent countless hours with ear, nose, and throat specialists; audiologists, speech and language therapists; and brain-training and reading specialists. It took a huge effort to find the right fit. But I did it, and miraculously, his hearing came back. I'm proud to say that he is now a sophomore in nursing school at Penn State.

The story I want to focus on in this chapter is about my son Christopher. I learned a great lesson from him that I would like to share.

Chris, now twenty-five and a junior executive for an investment company, was a normal kid who loved playing sports. But in sixth grade, Chris was diagnosed with Arthritic Lyme Disease. He had a swollen knee and was treated with Doxycycline for four weeks, which was the normal protocol. Prior to this, he had often fought leg pain, sometimes waking up at night screaming in agony. I was the only mother on the sideline of the soccer field with Bengay in her bag for those occasions when the pain was too much for him to bear. Over the years, I mentioned this to his doctors, but they didn't find it alarming. Instead, they instructed me to increase his milk and/or potassium intake.

After Chris was treated for Lyme, he seemed more exhausted and his eyes were always glassy. His pediatrician decided to run a few more tests, which revealed an extremely high level of creatine kinase (CK) in his blood. This meant that Chris's muscles were deteriorating, but we didn't know why or how he could be helped. Chris urgently needed to be seen at CHOP, a place familiar to me from my other son's struggle with Eczema. At CHOP, Chris went through a battery of tests. After the tests were complete, the specialists said it appeared as if Chris had Muscular Dystrophy. But he was physically too high-performing for them to make that diagnosis and were therefore unsure about how to guide us.

DMD is the largest known human gene, one that provides instructions for making a protein called dystrophin. This protein is located primarily in muscles used for movement (skeletal muscles), and in the heart (cardiac) muscle. Small amounts of dystrophin are present in nerve cells in the brain. But back in 2006, only approximately 70% of the entire dystrophin gene had been mapped out. One doctor told me to think of the dystrophin gene as a book with 72 chapters in it. If you have Muscular Dystrophy, you either have deleted chapters, or something called a stop codon that won't allow you to read past it. This is why the doctors were at a loss.

I kept going back to Lyme Disease. *Did this somehow cause the increase in Chris's CK level?* The doctors couldn't say. They did say, however, that his muscles were deteriorating, but they didn't know why. One of the best hospitals in the world was stumped. I couldn't just stand by and do nothing, so I started looking for answers elsewhere. Over the next year and a half, Chris and I traveled to several doctors, most of whom were Lyme Disease specialists. Still no answers, but I persisted. If there was a course of action that would stop further deteriorration, I was going to find it.

It wasn't until Chris was fifteen that we got a fateful phone call.

It was the kind of moment when time slows down and you can feel your heart beating. I heard the voice of my son's doctor on the line, and, as he spoke, chills ran up my spine. I knew our lives would never be the same.

"Medical science has finally mapped out the entire DMD gene," the doctor told me. "We know with certainty that Chris has Muscular Dystrophy. You need to come in as soon as possible."

When we got to CHOP, they told us that based on Christopher's previous results, this revelation was unexpected. The experts assumed that the beginning of the gene was the most important section, and Chris's doctors had discovered that his mutation was a stop codon on the first chapter. In other words, he should not be alive.

If what they thought was true, it meant that his body wasn't getting any of the protein dystrophin, in which case his muscles should not be able to repair themselves. His body was obviously getting around this. But how?

Muscular Dystrophy is a degenerative disease. As Chris and I sat in the doctors' waiting room, we saw kids who were suffering devastating effects. We thanked God that Chris's condition was not that bad, at least not yet. Overall, he was performing normally.

Since Muscular Dystrophy is a disease linked to the X chromosome, I was asked to do a blood test. That showed that I have the same mutation as Chris, making me a carrier. Then we had my parents tested, and found out that my dad also has the disease. At seventy-three, he became CHOP's oldest patient. He had miraculously lived a normal life that included playing sports as a child, and serving in the Army as a young man.

We were also told that several other people across the United States had been found to have the same mutation. As it turns out, they are relatives of ours from eight to ten generations back, originating in Western Europe. We were a geneticist's dream. The doctors could not contain their excitement at the discovery that cast doubt on what they had believed to be true about the gene. We happily signed over Christopher's biopsies to be donated for testing. It was important to figure out why his body was able to get around the codon, in hopes that other kids could experience the same relief.

Chris's doctors had asked him before if he'd ever experienced "Coca-Cola colored" urine. The answer had always been no. Incredibly, the day after we got the call from the doctor, this changed. Chris was playing ninth-grade lacrosse at his local high school. His coach caught him walking instead of running to the huddle, most likely because his legs hurt. As punishment, the coach sent him to run the track. As Chris ran, the coach became distracted and forgot about him. Chris continued running until he was finally told to stop; the coach apologized when he realized his lapse. When Chris got home, his urine was Coca-Cola colored. What this meant was that his kidneys could not process the muscle waste. If it continued, the doctors told us, he would need a kidney transplant.

Chris was advised to drop competitive team sports, and limit his activity to swimming, biking, and yoga. This was a big blow for a teenage boy with a passion for sports. Chris was on the high school soccer and lacrosse teams and did not want to tell anyone at school about his diagnosis. I felt terrible for him; his identity was built around sports. My son was about to encounter big changes in his life, and as his mother, I felt helpless.

We also had our other three boys to worry about. Since I was a carrier, they had a 50/50 chance of inheriting the disease. When they were tested, Chris's brothers learned that they are all free of the disease. Our daughter, the youngest of my children, could not be tested because she was under 18. Legally she must reach adulthood before requesting the test. My siblings and other family were tested as well, and we learned that the son of one of my sisters has the disease.

I was still terrified: *What did this mean for Chris's future?* Among those identified with the mutation in the nationwide study, there was a teenager in a wheelchair, an adult who had gone into a wheelchair at age forty, and of course, my father. *Why the difference in gene expression?* There was no clear answer. I went through many emotions as I processed Chris's diagnosis; denial and fear were among them. I also felt guilty for passing on this gene, even though I'd been unaware of its existence. I wondered about Chris's future children, along with his heart, muscle deterioration, and mental state in dealing with it all.

My illusion of being able to protect my children began to crumble. This was our new reality, and I felt unsteady and vulnerable. As I worried about how Chris would cope with his diagnosis, he taught me a lesson. We were driving in the car and I asked him if he wanted to speak with someone professional about his feelings. He looked at me for a moment and emphatically said, "I will consider that someday when my body falls apart. Right now, I am going to live like I am fine. Yes, my life has to change somewhat, but for now, I am walking. So I am good."

Chris's courage and strength in that moment were amazing. His words of wisdom have replayed in my mind many times. He was brave and profound to be positive about the hand he had been dealt. I gained strength from his attitude, and began reframing the situation in my own mind. I had to let go of the boy I thought I had – and also the illusion that I could protect my kids from bad things. I had to accept that this was a degenerative disease, and that I had no control over the outcome.

I needed to let go. I needed to let my son handle this his own way.

We stayed on top of doctors' appointments and educated ourselves on the disease. We did yoga, with Chris getting his heart checked regularly. Chris was learning to trust his body and manage his own health. Only he would know if he was doing too much.

Chris has managed his health throughout high school, college, and beyond. He decided to take up distance running, and I watched him run his first marathon in April 2017, his fiancé by his side. They do half-marathons as well. Chris has made a conscious choice about how he wants to live his life. There are so many lessons to be learned from his choice, and I am grateful for his example.

Life is in a constant state of change, giving us many opportunities to let go. If something in your life is not strengthening you, or bringing you joy and peace, it is time to release it. Ask yourself: Am I hanging on to this a little too long, like the infant with the rattle? If so, breathe and let it go. *But how?*

Eastern philosophies offer wisdom on the topic of letting go. In particular, Buddhist teachings on non-attachment are based on realizing one's own truth. We cling to our expectations of how the world – our world – is supposed to work. When reality diverges from our expectations, we confront pain, struggle, and the inability to find peace. In my coaching practice, I have helped people let go of negativity in the form of bad habits, beliefs, behaviors, thoughts, and relationships. We must release what no longer serves our purpose. As Yoda told Luke Skywalker, "Train yourself to let go of everything you fear to lose."

Today, my son Christopher is thriving, and our family is stronger for having gone through this experience. I have accepted that my life continues to evolve. And as it does, I breathe through the changes.

About the Authors

Meri Har-Gil

Meri Har-Gil started her career as a spa owner twenty-five years ago, working closely with women as their unofficial coach and sounding board. Her own success motivated her to become the inspiring Life and Business Coach that she is today. In producing Volumes I and II of the *Who's Going To Stop Us Now?* series, Meri's vision was to bring together a group of inspiring women who have overcome adversity and have their own stories of triumph to share. *Lessons In Letting Go* demonstrates Meri's passion for encouraging people to achieve their dreams, one step at a time.

To contact Meri, email her at merihargil@yahoo.ca

KEREN BARANES ABU

Keren Baranes Abu is a self-motivated entrepreneur who was born and raised in Israel. She immigrated to Canada with her husband and young daughter in 2008. In her chapter entitled, *Designing Happiness*, Keren describes her youth in which she lived a life of financial uncertainty, ultimately motivating her to seek out the Canadian dream of a better future. Today, Keren and her husband are the successful owners of an award winning architectural landscape design company, which they built together from the ground up, literally!

To contact Keren, email her at keren.eitana@gmail.com

JULLY BLACK

Jully Black is an international recording artist, songwriter and performer. She has collaborated with industry heavyweights such as Destiny's Child and Sean Paul. She has shared the stage with superstars such as Celine Dion, Elton John and Etta James, to name a few.

With purpose driven ideals and boundless spiritual fortitude, Jully continues to refine and reinvent her artistry. A phenom in Canadian entertainment, lifestyle and public speaking arenas, she is co-founder and key note speaker for the renowned "Empowered In My Skin" women's empowerment summits, a Notable.ca award recipient, and a WE Day ambassador.

Through music, spirituality and motivational speaking, helping everyone become his or her greater self is what Jully does. Being a bridge big enough for everyone to cross is who Jully *is*.

Ruth Cohen

Ruth Cohen, M.S.W., R.S.W., is a clinical social worker who grew up in Montreal. Ruth obtained an Honours B.A. in psychology in 1992 and her graduate degree from the University of Toronto in 1994. Ruth has been registered with the Ontario College of Social Workers and Social Service Workers since 2000, after leaving a career in child protection and entering children's mental health. Ruth has over 20 years of experience working with children and families throughout Ontario, as well internationally, in London, England. In the past decade, Ruth has focused her attention on empowering women to escape from high-conflict relationships and helping them break their silence in speaking out against domestic violence.

Ruth is a full-time single mother who is constantly inspired by her daughter's tenacity and perseverance to overcome life's challenges. She is an animal lover and advocate in educating others on type 1 diabetes, which her daughter manages on a daily basis.

Ruth can be reached at ruthiecohen@icloud.com

MARLA DAVID

Marla David is a Life Coach, speaker, co-author of five #1 International Bestselling compilations (Empowering Women to Succeed Volume II: From Burnout to Victory and Volume III: Bounce, 365 Moments of Grace and 365 Life Shifts, and The Sisterhood Folios: Live Out Loud). Marla has certifications including TESOL (Teaching English as a Second Language), NLP Practitioner, Law of Attraction Basic Practitioner, Ericksonian Hypnosis, Coach in Life Optimization, Master Life Coach, Basic Hypnotic Communicator, Coach Practitioner, Reiki I and Reiki II, and The Passion Test Facilitator. Marla shares her skills, paying it forward where she can. She is an advocate for women, children, and animals, and is a member of *Women for Nature* (Nature Canada), furthering her love of nature (and her Facebook page Roses and Rainbows). A mom of three grown daughters, and a new grandmother, Marla lives her life of passion each and every day, spending time with family and friends, her dogs, and enjoying travel, arts, and culture.

Debbie Doolittle

Debbie Doolittle navigated through a childhood in which she felt her needs were very low on the proverbial totem pole. It took until her teen years to really find a sense of purpose, and after doing so, she became a highly sought after hair stylist. She is now the owner of a large, and very successful beauty salon.

Serving as a friend and confidant to thousands of clients has brought Debbie immense satisfaction over the years. She's also proud to have created a workplace that offers her employees opportunities to pursue their own professional and personal development goals. However, it is her training as a trauma and PTSD life coach that has really elevated Debbie to a whole new level of professional fulfillment.

To contact Debbie, email her at debbie@ptsdtransformationslifecoach.com

CHRISTIE ECHEVERRI

Christie Echeverri is a freelance writer and editor, mother of two, and bargain enthusiast living in Portland, Oregon. She studied American History at The University of Hawaii, with a minor in Self-deprecation. She enjoys family, food, football, feelings, and floppy-eared dogs. Christie is passionate about mental health advocacy, with the recent loss of her mother hastening her resolve to live a kinder, more authentic life.

To contact Christie, email her at strugalugging@gmail.com or find her at www.strugalug.com

Angie Fix

Angie Fix was born in Uganda and raised in Canada. Her passion for humanity from an early age led her to a lengthy, successful career in health care. Being raised in a traditional family she often took a stand against social norms allowing her to lend support and courage to those in similar circumstances. Her mantra is, "respect everyone and everything in your environment but most importantly start with respecting yourself." Her interests include yoga, nature walks, and meditation. Today, in addition to her career in health care, Angie Fix is a Reiki Master Practitioner and a medium. She believes the world needs more love and compassion and each one of us is capable of making it a better place. Her philosophy is, in order to lead an authentic life we must first remove the plastic layers and return "Back to Basics." Her greatest accomplishment has been raising her two beautiful children - an honour she doesn't take for granted.

ORIT GAL

Orit ("Light" in Hebrew) Gal, was born in Israel and currently resides in Sharon, Ontario. As a young girl, Orit dreamed of becoming an educator and children's rights advocate. After joining the Israeli Defense Army and serving in the Navy, Orit became a kindergarten teacher. Years later, she pursued her Canadian dream by opening three childcare centers. Becoming an entrepreneur was so empowering for her that she felt inspired to help other women achieve the same kind of financial independence. Orit now runs Early Education Childcare Center Development, a company that helps women become their own boss. She and her husband are the proud parents of two daughters and two sons.

Orit can be reached at 416-500-5041, or early.educa@gmail.com

Jaime Lund Onofrey

Jaime Lund Onofrey is an agent of change in a wild new world. Her passion for breaking through old constructs to make way for new possibility stems from three near death experiences.

Chinese Medicine, Ayurvedic Philosophy, Meditation, and the study of the power of conscious co-creation, have laid the foundation for a life devoted to helping others awaken to their souls purpose.

After graduating from Film Production and being mentored by some of the best business and personal development minds on the planet, Jaime is now emerging as a new thought leader in her own right.

Her vision for the expansion of human potential and our birthright to thrive, puts her at the forefront of the new wild-west. Jaime, along with other change makers, are braving this new frontier, as our global family seeks to find what unites us, as oppose to what separates us.

Find her at: www.thrivetribe.tv

MARIA REDA GOLDSTEIN

Maria Reda Goldstein is a native New Yorker who grew up in Montreal, Quebec and later moved to Toronto. She speaks English, French, Italian and a little Spanish. She fell into the insurance industry in 1980 and is currently a Registered Insurance Broker specializing in boat insurance.

Maria is the eldest of four children. Following in the footsteps of their late father, her three brothers also work in the insurance industry. She has been married to the love of her life since 2003, who coincidentally, is also an insurance broker. Although she calls Toronto her home, Maria visits Montreal a couple of times a year with her husband. In her personal time, Maria enjoys reading, good movies, entertaining and travelling.

To contact Maria, email her at mariareda@gmail.com

NELL ROSE FOREMAN

Nell Rose Foreman believes your mind is your greatest tool for success. She has trained everyone from athletes to corporate titans on how to take control of their minds and overcome the limiting beliefs and fears that hold them back from their true potential. As a board certified coach and certified hypnotherapist, Nell Rose has helped her clients overcome obstacles for over a decade. Her talents, however, don't stop with the mind. Her techniques focus on optimizing mindset for peak performance.

Nell Rose is also certified in Neuro-Linguistic Programming, one of the fastest and most effective ways to create lasting psychological change by utilizing strategies based in neuroscience. She is a successful entrepreneur, Amazon International best-selling author, and popular keynote speaker. Most importantly, she is a dedicated mother to her five children (and three furry children), in Malvern, PA.

To contact Nell Rose, email her at nellrose5@gmail.com

www.ingramcontent.com/pod-product-compliance
Lightning Source LLC
Chambersburg PA
CBHW070452100426
42743CB00010B/1583